THE STORIES OF JESUS' BIRTH

The Stories of Jesus' Birth

A CRITICAL INTRODUCTION

Edwin D. Freed

St. Louis, Missouri

To all students and others who participated in or will participate in discussions of the subject of this book

Published by
Sheffield Academic Press Ltd
Mansion House, 19 Kingfield Road
Sheffield S11 9AS
England

www.SheffieldAcademicPress.com

ISBN 1 84127 132 2

Published in the USA and Canada (only) by
Chalice Press
PO Box 179
St Louis, MO 63166-0179
USA

www.ChalicePress.com

USA and Canada only
ISBN 0-8272-3451-1

Typeset by Sheffield Academic Press
and
Printed on acid-free paper in Great Britain
by The Cromwell Press
Trowbridge, Wiltshire

British Library Cataloguing-in-Publication Data
A catalogue record for this book is available
from the British Library

Library of Congress Cataloging-in-Publication Data
A catalog record for this book is available from the Library of Congress

CONTENTS

PREFACE

This work was conceived long ago but written after many years of discussions on the so-called Christmas stories with college students, church members in Christian education courses, and other study groups. Most persons seemed to appreciate the observations we made and the questions we raised and discussed freely and openly. Therefore, this book is written for a broad spectrum of readers, including college and theological students, church study groups, other interested lay people, and clergy.

As the subtitle is meant to indicate, the book is only an introduction to the most important aspects and problems in the study of the stories of Jesus' birth from a critical perspective. But readers not trained in critical scholarship should not be turned off by the words 'critical' and 'criticism'. Some readers may think of the word 'critical' in the negative sense of finding fault or disapproving. However, when used in biblical studies it has a positive meaning. The word criticism comes from the Greek verb *krino*, meaning to 'separate', 'distinguish', 'choose', 'decide' or 'judge'. Therefore, whenever we study a subject critically, we judge between alternatives and try to decide which is the best solution to the problem under consideration on the basis of evidence or lack of it.

Readers will find a perspective on the stories of Jesus' birth that differs from that of persons who approach the subject from various doctrinal points of view. The book is intended to challenge all readers who are willing to go beyond denominational and romantic approaches to the study of Jesus to think as objectively as possible about the interesting but perplexing accounts in the first two chapters of Matthew and Luke. The aim is to inform and to educate, not to convert, divert or indoctrinate anyone.

This book will be most appreciated by readers whose brains are not stuffed with preconceived notions and stale opinions, but have room for different ideas and intellectual challenges. The minds in such brains will have room for the opinions of others in order more clearly to formulate their own. The ultimate outcome of critical study will always be a willingness to make a habit of considering alternatives and not to take the usual views for granted.

My method is intentionally repetitive. I introduce you to a section of material and then later deal with it again for more detailed study and with something added for further thought. Sometimes I will state my opinion and sometimes I won't, because on some questions there is not enough evidence to form a conclusive opinion. I hope all readers will be challenged to consider the stories of Jesus' birth more carefully than ever before.

Since this work was written in its earliest form, several important books have appeared that deal with the stories of Jesus' birth, and I sometimes deal with them on various aspects of this subject. In different ways I have learned something from each of the authors mentioned, and I hope that as you read this work you will also learn from them. Their works are an excellent basic bibliography for any of you who may want to do more advanced study of any aspect of the stories of Jesus' birth.

The encyclopedic and definitive work on the stories of Jesus' birth is that of Professor Raymond E. Brown, *The Birth of the Messiah.*[1] This new and updated volume is a massive, but delightfully written, work of 752 pages. I hope my much shorter volume will be useful for readers interested in the subject before they turn to Professor Brown's book for further study.

Over the span of many years, I have learned much from Professor Brown on many subjects of New Testament study, including the one treated in this book, which, by the way, is not a condensation or rewriting of Professor Brown's work. I have gone off on my own way, and most of what I say is based on years of teaching and study long before that work appeared. At the same time, if my book has aroused your interest, I urge you to consult Brown's volume for every aspect of this study.

The second work is that of Joseph A. Fitzmyer, *The Gospel According to Luke.*[2] This work is important for its attention to the Greek lan-

1. *The Birth of the Messiah: A Commentary on the Infancy Narratives in the Gospels of Matthew and Luke* (ABRL; New York: Doubleday, 1993).

2. *The Gospel According to Luke* (2 vols.; AB, 28, 28A; Garden City, NY: Doubleday, 1981, 1985), I, pp. 287-448.

guage of Luke, the Old Testament background of the birth narratives, its insightful translation and commentary, and extensive bibliographies on all aspects of Lukan studies.

As usual, the volumes of Michael D. Goulder, *Luke: A New Paradigm*,[3] the third work, is distinctive and provocative. It is distinctive in that its author believes Luke got the germ of the idea for the organization of his first two chapters from Mark, and that his birth stories were not written independently of Matthew but based on his Gospel. I never fail to learn something new from Professor Goulder's books.

The fourth work is by Richard A. Horsley, *The Liberation of Christmas*.[4] Its distinctiveness is indicated in the subtitle: 'The Infancy Narratives in Social Context'. The theme is that the 'Christmas' narratives are stories of liberation of all the Jewish people from socioeconomic, political and religious oppression. While acknowledging Horsley's contribution to our understanding of the social context of the stories, I place more emphasis on the religious aspects of the stories themselves.

Unless stated otherwise, the translations of passages from the Bible are those of the NRSV and are used by permission. The translations from other writings are mostly my own, although for Greek and Roman authors I sometimes follow closely those in the Loeb Classical Library, from which references are taken. Translations from the Talmuds and Midrash are taken from the standard English editions listed in the bibliography.

Finally, I want to thank my wife Ann for working seemingly endless hours to help me in many ways so that I am free to work on projects such as this one. And for this work she has helped me in many ways, especially with the proofreading.

3. *Luke: A New Paradigm* (2 vols.; JSNTSup, 20; Sheffield: JSOT Press, 1989).

4. *The Liberation of Christmas: The Infancy Narratives in Social Context* (New York: Crossroad, 1989), pp. 1-123.

ABBREVIATIONS

AB	Anchor Bible
ABRL	Anchor Bible Reference Library
EncJud	*Encyclopaedia Judaica*
JSNT	*Journal for the Study of the New Testament*
JSNTSup	*Journal for the Study of the New Testament*, Supplement Series
LCL	Loeb Classical Library
NRSV	New Revised Standard Version
NTS	*New Testament Studies*
OTP	James Charlesworth (ed.), *Old Testament Pseudepigrapha*
REB	*Revised English Bible*
TS	*Theological Studies*

INTRODUCTION

Except for the first two chapters of Matthew and Luke, there is no hint of Jesus' birth from a virgin anywhere in the New Testament. But please turn to the beginning of Luke's genealogy of Jesus in Lk. 3.23 and notice the words 'as was thought'. These words indicate that some people did believe that Jesus was actually the son of Joseph. At the same time, though, the words imply that there were other people who thought that Jesus was not Joseph's son. Those who thought Jesus was not Joseph's son apparently were aware of the tradition of the virgin birth of Jesus. So it appears that either Luke himself, who believed Jesus was the son of Joseph (see Lk. 2.33, 41-52; 4.22; cf. Mk 6.3 and Mt. 13.55), or a later scribe added the words 'as was thought' to Luke's genealogy of Jesus in order to make it coincide with the story of Jesus' miraculous conception by a virgin as reported in the infancy narratives.

Paul, whose letters are the earliest writings in the New Testament, speaks of Jesus as physically descended from David (Rom. 1.3) but mentions the actual birth of Jesus only in Gal. 4.4. The scant information in Paul's letters and the silence of Mark, the earliest Gospel, and of the Gospel of John concerning Jesus' birth are not insignificant. For those and other reasons the stories of Jesus' birth are probably among the latest traditions that developed about Jesus and among the last materials to be incorporated in the Gospels. However, there are no known manuscripts of Matthew and Luke without the birth narratives and no manuscripts of Mark that have them.

In view of what we have learned thus far, how then can we explain the different beliefs about Jesus' birth and lineal descent?

From Christology to the Birth of Jesus

Christology is a modern term scholars use in discussing beliefs about Jesus. It comes from two Greek words: *christos* (English, 'Christ'), meaning 'anointed one', and *logos*, meaning 'word'. Literally, then,

Christology is the word about Christ as the anointed one or Messiah or, more specifically, the things believed and taught about him by Christians.

At the beginning of this study of the stories of Jesus' birth we should be aware that when used in conjunction with the study of Jesus, the term 'Christians' is an anachronism. During the time of Jesus there were no persons known by that name, which became a designation for followers of Jesus rather long after his death. Moreover, as far as I know, the term Christianity was used for the first time by Ignatius, Bishop of Antioch, who was martyred early in the second century AD. In his *Letter to the Magnesians* (10.3) he uses the term 'Christianity' in distinction from Judaism and says that everyone who believed in God was brought into it. So the designation 'followers of Jesus' would be more appropriate than the term Christians. But for the sake of convenience I sometimes also use the anachronistic terms Christians and Christianity.

Followers of Jesus used several designations when referring to themselves. The earliest one was probably 'brothers', a word Paul uses in every letter when referring to fellow believers. In fact, 'believers' was also used among early followers of Jesus to distinguish faithful Jews or pagans as converts to the Jesus movement from persons who were not (see Acts 2.44; 4.32; see also 1 Thess. 1.7-8; 2.10, 13). Believers were not to participate in the immoral practices of unbelievers but were to cleanse themselves 'from every defilement of body and of spirit, making holiness perfect in the fear of God' (2 Cor. 7.1; see also 2 Cor. 6.14-16). It is not surprising, then, that Jesus was proclaimed as holy even before his birth (Lk. 1.35, 49; see also 2.23).

The word 'holiness' brings us to the third, and perhaps the most significant, designation used by the first followers of Jesus to refer to themselves. That is 'holy ones' (*hagioi*), usually translated as 'saints'. It is Paul's characteristic form of address when referring to the recipients of his letters (1 Cor. 1.2; 2 Cor. 1.1; Rom. 1.7; Phil. 1.1; Phlm 5; see also Acts 9.13, 32, 41; 26.10). Thus, it was no accident that 'believers' and 'holy ones' were the prevailing words used to distinguish followers of Jesus from others in the polytheistic social world of early New Testament times. From the beginning, faithfulness toward God, beliefs about Jesus, and moral life were inseparably linked together. See here key passages in 1 Thessalonians, Paul's earliest letter, especially 1 Thess. 1.5-10; 3.11-13. We should expect, then, that followers of

Jesus would believe he was proclaimed as holy even before his birth (Lk. 1.35, 49; see also Lk. 2.23).

Now that we have taken ourselves briefly back into the time of Jesus' first followers, we must remember what we have learned as we think about how the tradition concerning Jesus' birth probably developed.

Development of Traditions

Perhaps the tradition of Jesus' unique birth developed somewhat in the following manner. Early Jewish followers of Jesus first came to believe that he was their long-expected Messiah (Christ) and combined the title Christ with his given name Jesus (see Mt. 1.21, 25; Lk. 1.31; 2.21, 27, 43). The title appears with the name in Paul's letters in the form Jesus Christ (e.g. 1 Thess. 1.1, 3; Rom. 1.1, 4; 2.16; Phil. 1.11; Mk 1.1; Mt. 1.16, 18) or Christ Jesus (e.g. 1 Thess. 2.14; 5.18; 1 Cor. 1.1; 2 Cor. 1.1; Gal. 2.4; Eph. 1.1).

Next, some followers of Jesus became convinced that their Messiah had risen from the dead, and then they tried to show that his resurrection had been predicted in the Hebrew scriptures (cf. 1 Cor. 15.4 with Hos. 6.2 and Mt. 12.39-40 with Jon. 2.1). Such followers of Jesus then came to believe that Jesus himself had predicted his resurrection from the dead. A good example of such a prediction is Lk. 24.46, where Luke reports that Jesus says: 'Thus it is written, that the Messiah is to suffer and to rise from the dead on the third day' (see Hos. 6.2; Jon. 2.1; see also Mk 10.32-34; Mt. 27.62-63; Lk. 24.6-7).

Finally, it was only natural, I suppose, that Jesus' devout followers came to believe that he must also have had a supernatural birth. However, the belief that Jesus rose from the dead was stronger and thus more enduring than the one about his miraculous conception and birth. This is true because the belief in Jesus' miraculous birth, as we have learned, is rarely mentioned in the New Testament. On the other hand, the belief in Jesus' resurrection is prominent throughout the New Testament.

Jewish-Christian Beliefs about Jesus and the Gentiles

Since Christianity began within Judaism, most of Jesus' first followers were Jews. Eventually they began to preach their message that Jesus was the Messiah to other Jews and non-Jews, or Gentiles. Gentiles, however, were not expecting a political redeemer, a messiah ('anointed one'), much less a crucified one.

In Hebrew society a particular man, who had previously been approved by God to be ruler of the people, was anointed with oil by a priest or prophet to be king. According to 1 Sam. 10.1, 'Samuel took a vial of oil and poured it on his [Saul's] head, and kissed him; he said, "The Lord has anointed you ruler over his people Israel".' The king, therefore, was often referred to as 'the Lord's anointed' (e.g. 1 Sam. 12.3; 16.6; 24.6; 2 Sam. 1.14; 19.21).

Greeks and Romans thought of oil as something used for rubbing sore muscles of athletes, not for pouring on the heads of political rulers. Obviously, the title 'Messiah' would mean nothing to them. Moreover, non-Jews were used to thinking of gods, sons of gods, lords, and even saviors. Consequently, followers of Jesus used the titles 'Son of God' and 'Lord' with reference to Jesus in an effort to win converts among Gentiles, as well as among non-believing Jews, to their beliefs about Jesus and to their way of life as followers of him.

Not all followers of Jesus shared the same beliefs concerning Jesus, for example, how or when he became Messiah, Son of God, and Lord. A diversity of views is reported in the book of Acts. The author writes: 'This Jesus God raised up... God has made him both Lord and Messiah, this Jesus whom you crucified' (Acts 2.32-36; allusions to Pss. 110.1; 2.2; 132.10). Here in Acts the author reflects the view that both 'Lord' and 'Messiah' were attributes ascribed to Jesus after his death and resurrection. In Acts 4.27 the author writes that Jesus was the one 'whom you anointed'. Here the 'you' is God, addressed in prayer; but when Jesus was anointed, the author does not say. In Acts 10.37-38 the anointing of Jesus is associated with his baptism (as in Mk 1.9-11): 'After the baptism that John announced: how God anointed Jesus of Nazareth with the Holy Spirit and with power'. This verse may be an allusion to Isa. 61.1, which Luke, also the author of Acts, quotes in Lk. 4.18: 'The Spirit of the Lord is upon me, because he has anointed me to bring good news to the poor'. This seems to indicate that Luke believed Jesus became the Messiah at his baptism. Or it may mean that Jesus was the Messiah before his birth, since he had been conceived through the Holy Spirit (Lk. 1.32-35). Luke may, though, have copied the passages in Acts from his sources. At any rate, the passages in Acts reflect different opinions among followers of Jesus about how he became or was made Messiah.

With respect to the sonship of Jesus, some followers of Jesus thought the title was bestowed upon him by God during his baptism. Mark writes that a voice came from heaven, saying: 'You are my Son, the Beloved [or 'my beloved Son']; with you I am well pleased' (Mk 1.9-11; see also Mt. 3.16-17; Lk. 3.21-22). Other followers of Jesus thought he became Son by virtue of his resurrection from the dead. That is the view of Paul: '[Jesus] was declared to be Son of God with power according to the spirit of holiness by resurrection from the dead' (Rom. 1.4). The same view is recorded in Acts 13.33.

It is important to know that the most characteristic feature in the environment of New Testament times was polytheism. Greeks and Romans in general believed in the existence of many gods, lords and saviors. Such polytheism was the greatest threat to the development of Christianity as a religion separate from Judaism. Why is this true? Because most converts to the developing religion, which later became known as Christianity, were Gentiles. Most of them were accustomed to worshiping several gods and participating in pagan, often immoral, religious practices. For that reason Paul, still the Jewish monotheist, taught the members of his churches to believe that there was 'no God but one...one God, the Father...and one Lord, Jesus Christ' (1 Cor. 8.4). Paul wanted the converts in every church to believe that Jesus Christ was '*the* Lord' (1 Thess. 1.1; 1 Cor. 1.3; 2 Cor. 1.2; Gal. 1.3; Phil. 1.2; Rom. 1.7; Phlm 1.3) and to acknowledge him as '*our* Lord' (1 Thess. 1.3; 1 Cor. 1.2; 2 Cor. 1.3; Rom. 1.4; see also Eph. 1.2; Col. 2.6; 2 Thess. 1.1, 8). The beliefs in Jesus as Son of God, Lord and Savior are present in the stories of Jesus' birth (Mt. 1.21; 2.15; Lk. 1.35, 43, 68, 76; 2.11, 30, 49).

After followers of Jesus of Nazareth came to believe that he was not only the Messiah but also Son of God, Lord and Savior, it was only natural that some should also believe that he had a supernatural origin. That view is represented by the persons who composed the stories of Jesus' birth. But just how unique was the birth of Jesus? I shall turn to that question later, but let me first say that the final step in the Christians' understanding of Jesus as divine, even God, is to be found in the fourth Gospel, the Gospel of John. The author of that Gospel believed that Jesus had always existed: 'In the beginning was the Word, and the Word was with God, and the Word was God. He was in the beginning with God' (Jn 1.1-2).

Since the author of the fourth Gospel believed that Jesus had always existed, it would be inconceivable for him to believe that Jesus was conceived and born even in a supernatural way. Jesus simply assumed human form: 'And the Word became flesh and lived among us' (Jn 1.14). See Paul's statement in Gal. 4.4: 'But when the fullness of time had come, God sent his Son, born of a woman'. Here, according to Paul, Jesus was God's Son before his birth.

Legend, Myth, History

At this point it would be helpful for you to read Mt. 1.18-25, Lk. 1.26-38 and 2.1-7.

I turn now to the stories of Jesus' unique birth. Or should I say the unique stories of Jesus' birth (Mt. 1.1–2.23; Lk. 1.5–2.52)? The stories are rather unique in the way they present insights into the theological viewpoints of their composers.[1] They are, indeed, compositions that contain inspirational prose and poetry with a truly musical quality, as has long been recognized.

Some scholars regard the stories of Jesus' birth as legends or myths. Perhaps readers unaccustomed to the critical study of the Bible may think of legends and myths as nasty words always to be avoided, especially when studying stories about Jesus. But persons who want to become enlightened students of the Bible need not think of legends and myths as pejorative terms when used in biblical studies of any kind, including those about Jesus.

Religious legends develop when some people take a special interest in a good person and then write nice stories about that person. Such people may think of the good person as one whose life, works and destiny are determined by the gods or God. Sometimes legends may contain some historical content.

Stories that deal with the interactions of the gods and human beings are usually regarded as myths.[2] As with legends, myths develop around special or unusual persons, who may even be regarded as supernatural. Myths are often highly imaginative and unbelievable in the ways they portray the behavior and events associated with unusual persons. The purpose of myths is not to convey historical facts but to explain practices, beliefs or natural phenomena in a meaningful way for the persons who hear or read the myths. With respect to the narratives of Jesus' birth, for example, the writer probably did not intend the story about the

1. Here I am closer to the views of Brown and Goulder than to those of Horsley (*Liberation*, pp. 6-9).

2. For further study of myth see Horsley, *Liberation*, pp. 1-6.

baby Jesus in the manger (Lk. 2.6-7) to be taken literally. Rather, the writer wanted to convey vividly the humble origins of Jesus.

Horsley proposes 'a concept of realistic or history-like narrative' for adequately understanding the stories of Jesus' birth. According to Horsley, in order to do that we must seek the subject matter or meaning only in a narrative itself and to understand it 'against the historical background of its origin and reference'.[3] Most scholars nowadays, I believe, try to do that, although sometimes from different perspectives, with different emphases and presuppositions.

Even with a cursory reading of the birth narratives we observe immediately that there are differences between the accounts of Matthew and Luke. Differences appear even in places where there are likenesses. These differences make the enlightened reader skeptical of the historical veracity of some, even many, of the things that are written.

With respect to the content of the stories of Jesus' birth, the historical validity of some of the material was questioned as early as the second century. In the birth narratives we are, indeed, confronted with problems of some magnitude. That fact is all the more reason why we should study the narratives critically and try to provide some likely answers to the problems.

The basic question, it seems to me, is this: What are the most likely explanations for the origin of the stories? In trying to answer that question we have to deal with others. How much of the material in the stories comes from earlier sources Matthew and Luke may have used? On the other hand, how much of it did each writer himself alter or even compose? And why did each writer use the material he found in his sources? Or if each author composed some material himself, why did he do so?

I hope you will find the method I use in the study of the stories of Jesus' birth, perhaps well known to some of you, interesting and that you will gain some new insights into those religiously enlightened narratives.

With these topics as introductory background, I turn now to the actual stories of Jesus' birth. Because Matthew begins his Gospel with the genealogy of Jesus, I begin with Matthew's account.

3. Horsley, *Liberation*, pp. 18-19.

Chapter 1

The Genealogies of Jesus

Introductory Comments about the Genealogies

There may have been some genealogical lists of Jesus' ancestors before those of Matthew and Luke. Such lists would have been composed by persons other than those who wrote the rest of the birth narratives. Because of the differences in the genealogies as they appear in Matthew and Luke, it may be that they stem from different sources. The inexplicable differences in content and the different methods used in recording the genealogies may indicate that Matthew and Luke worked independently of each other in dealing with them.[1]

Whereas Matthew places the genealogy at the beginning of his Gospel, Luke inserts it as a sequel to Jesus' baptism. In that position it comes between the Markan account of the baptism of Jesus and his temptations by the devil in the wilderness. By inserting the genealogy at that place Luke has acted very cleverly. According to Luke, the angel Gabriel had promised Mary that Jesus would be called 'the Son of the Most High' (Lk. 1.32). According to Luke, God acknowledges Jesus in Mark's very words: 'You are my Son, the Beloved' (Lk. 3.22; Mk 1.11). Then as Son of God Jesus was tested by the devil: 'If you are the Son of God, command this stone to become a loaf of bread'. Jesus' reply shows that he had passed the test (Lk. 4.3-4).

Let me interject here a comment about a presupposition of this work. Notice that I have said that Luke uses 'Mark's very words'. This study presumes the still most widely accepted theory concerning the composition of the first three Gospels, the Synoptic Gospels. That theory—and it must be acknowledged as such—is that Mark was the first Gospel written and that in the composition of their Gospels Matthew and Luke

1. As Brown believes and Goulder does not, because Goulder thinks that Luke used Matthew creatively.

each used Mark and another common source called Q (from the German *Quelle*, 'source'), not used by Mark. And there is some material only in Matthew, for which scholars use the designation M, and some material only in Luke, which is designated L. There are problems with this theory—as with most theories—but we need not get into that here.

I return now to Luke and the Son of God. What Luke says about the Son of God in his Gospel agrees with his views in Acts, also written by Luke. According to Acts 9.20, Paul's first proclamation in the synagogues of Damascus was that Jesus 'is the Son of God'. And later in Athens Paul proclaims that 'God made the world and everything in it' and that, as with Adam and Jesus, 'we too are his offspring' (Acts 17.24, 28).

Although, following tradition, we use the word 'genealogies' with reference to the accounts of Mt. 1.1-17 and Lk. 3.23-38, the Greek term *genealogia* does not occur in either account. It occurs in the New Testament only in 1 Tim. 1.4 and Tit. 3.9. In 1 Tim. 1.4 the author warns his readers 'not to occupy themselves with myths and endless genealogies that promote speculations rather than the divine training that is known by faith'. Here the words genealogies and myths (Greek, *mythoi*) are used together. The same combination occurs in pagan Greek literature, for example, in Polybius (second century BC), *History* 9.2.1, where he writes 'concerning the genealogies and myths' in referring to the births of demigods and founders of certain cities. Thus, genealogies, as well as myths, were ancient literary types.

The writer of Tit. 3.9 exhorts his readers to 'avoid stupid controversies, genealogies, dissensions, and quarrels about the law, for they are unprofitable and worthless'. The very negative opinions about genealogies expressed in the passages quoted should caution us against attributing historical worth to those in Matthew and Luke. In light of such negative opinions, it seem strange, does it not, that the genealogies of Jesus even got into the New Testament.

Except for a few passages in the Gospels, Jesus as a descendant of David (as in the genealogies) was never an important belief for New Testament writers. The theologian who wrote the letter to the Hebrews argues that Jesus was a priest like Melchizedek (see Gen. 14.18; Ps. 110.4). Therefore, like that priest, Jesus had no genealogy. The author of Hebrews writes that Christ was the Son of God and eternal high priest. He was 'without father, without mother, without genealogy, having neither beginning of days nor end of life, but resembling the Son of God, he remains a priest forever' (recall Jn 1.1-2, 14, quoted above). But according to the author of Hebrews, Christ was not descended from the priests: 'He does not have their genealogy' (Heb. 7.6). The important thing in Hebrews is that, as with Aaron, Christ was called by God (Heb. 5.4; see Exod. 28.1). We might question whether the author of Hebrews was actually trying to negate the tradition about Jesus preserved in the genealogy, if not the stories of Jesus' birth themselves.

Jesus' Father and Grandfather

Perhaps one of the most interesting places to begin observing the problems that arise in the critical study of the genealogies of Jesus is with the reported (or 'supposed'?) grandfather of Jesus.

Although Matthew believed that the child conceived in Mary was 'from the Holy Spirit' (Mt. 1.20), he knew, of course, that God and the Holy Spirit produced no ancestral offspring whose genealogy could be traced through family lineage. Nor could there be a genealogy of Jesus if he had no human father. Obviously, Matthew saw nothing inconsistent or illogical in recording the descent of Jesus through Joseph (Mt. 1.16) and then immediately thereafter telling the story of the virgin Mary that clearly implies Joseph was not Jesus' biological father. Matthew says that the angel addressed Joseph as 'Joseph, son of David' (Mt. 1.20). There simply would be no point in referring to Joseph as a descendant of David unless the composer of the genealogy also believed his offspring were thereby also descended from David. As we have learned, it appears that an editor or a scribe—if not Luke himself—working with the genealogy in Luke's Gospel, was aware of the inconsistency. Familiar with the tradition of the virgin Mary, he inserted a parenthetical phrase before the name Joseph in the first sentence: 'He [Jesus] was the son (as was thought) of Joseph' (Lk. 3.23). Obviously, if Jesus had no human father, he would also not have had a grandfather.

An editor or scribe apparently also left his mark on Mt. 1.16. In keeping with the style in the whole genealogy, that verse probably originally read: 'Jacob the father of Joseph, and Joseph the father of Jesus'. The scribe, aware of the Mary legend, changed the text to read as it now stands: 'Jacob the father of Joseph the husband of Mary, of whom Jesus was born, who is called the Messiah [Christ]'.

Some later versions of Mt. 1.16 have different readings, for example: 'Jacob the father of Joseph. Joseph to whom the virgin Mary was betrothed, was the father of Jesus who is called the Christ.' This reading has the idea both ways: Joseph was the father of Jesus, and he was engaged to a virgin named Mary. The truth of the matter is that if Joseph did not beget Jesus the whole genealogy would be pointless and worthless. Jews readily understood this, as is evident in the genealogies in their scriptures. For example, in Gen. 5.1-32 the phrase 'he became the father of' is a recurring refrain. In Gen. 10.1-32 'the descendants of' are always listed after the name of the man who is the progenitor (see Gen. 11.10-27). According to a rabbinic saying in *B. Bat.* 2110b, 'The family on the father's side is called "family", but the family on the mother's side is not called "family" '.

I have said that the author of Hebrews writes that Jesus had neither father nor mother nor genealogy. So, of course, he would say nothing about a grandfather of Jesus. According to Mt. 1.16, Jacob was the grandfather of Jesus, but according to Lk. 3.23, Heli (Eli) was his grandfather. How is this difference to be explained? Jesus could not have had two paternal grandfathers, could he?

Brown resolves the difficulty by pointing to the theological viewpoints of Matthew and Luke. According to Brown, although we can use the genealogies to help evaluate Jesus, we learn nothing certain about his great grandparents or his grandparents. The message of Jesus as Joseph's son is not a factual matter with respect to his grandfather but 'theologically' that Jesus is 'son of David, son of Abraham' (Matthew), and 'Son of God' (Luke).[2]

On the other hand, Goulder sees the names in the genealogies as numerically significant and composed for symbolic reasons. He does not try to reconcile the problem of Jesus' grandfather. However, if I understand him correctly, Goulder takes Eli, the priest in Samuel's time, as one of the names symbolic of the priestly movement in Israel's history.[3]

At any rate, the names of Jesus' grandfather were hardly meant to be taken historically in the time of Matthew and Luke and even less so in our own. It appears that the writer of each genealogy manipulated the names for purposes not readily known to us. It is probably accurate to say that most scholars today agree that the names represent neither official records nor valued lists of ancestors.[4]

2. Brown, *Birth*, p. 94.
3. See Goulder, *Luke*, I, pp. 287-88.
4. See Fitzmyer, *Gospel*, I, p. 497.

The statement in Mt. 1.16 serves several purposes for Matthew. It makes Mary, instead of Joseph, the primary progenitor of Jesus, the Messiah. The reference to the Messiah, along with a similar reference in Mt. 1.17, prepares the reader for the account of 'the birth of Jesus the Messiah' that follows in Mt. 1.18-25. With the words, 'the account of the genealogy of Jesus the Messiah', in Mt. 1.1 Matthew has an appropriate introduction to the genealogy that he probably had before him when he wrote his Gospel.

Earlier I said that the word *genealogia* does not occur in the account of either Matthew or Luke. That is true in spite of the NRSV translation of the Greek phrase *biblos geneseōs* as 'the account of the genealogy of' in Mt. 1.1. The phrase is more properly translated as 'a record of the origin (or birth) of', and it takes the place of the words 'the beginning of the gospel of' in Mk 1.1. The phraseology shows influence from the Septuagint, the Greek translation of the Hebrew scriptures that is abbreviated LXX by scholars, because of the tradition that the translation was done by 70 sages. The phrase *biblos geneseōs* occurs in the LXX Gen. 2.4 and 5.1. I shall consider Matthew's first verse in more detail in Chapter 3 below.

With the words 'Jesus...who is called the Messiah' in Mt. 1.16 Matthew sets the genealogy off as an *inclusio*. *Inclusio* is a Latin word meaning 'a shutting up' or 'confinement'. In a passage of scripture, when a phrase or an idea in the opening line is repeated at the end, the section in between is an *inclusio*. Thus, by using 'the genealogy of Jesus the Messiah' in Mt. 1.1 and 'Jesus...who is called the Messiah' in Mt. 1.16 Matthew confines the genealogy he was working with to the material between those verses. This inclusion helps us to determine the limits of the genealogy. The statement in Mt. 1.17 about the generations of descendants is Matthew's own comment and not a part of the genealogy he was working with.

Son of David

Son of David is one of Matthew's favorite titles for Jesus, and he uses it more often in the body of his Gospel than Mark and Luke together. So it appears that Matthew is especially concerned with presenting Jesus as the Son of David.

Matthew had probably read the beginning of Mark's Gospel: 'The beginning of the good news (or gospel) of Jesus Christ, the Son of God' (Mk 1.1). If he had, did he use his phrases 'the son of David, the son of

Abraham' (Mt. 1.1) instead of Mark's 'the Son of God'? Some ancient manuscripts of Mark, though, lack 'the Son of God'. At any rate, Matthew must have had a reason for using the phrases as a part of the prelude to his stories of Jesus' birth. Let us see what his reason may have been.

With Matthew's use of the expression 'Son of David' we get a clue to one of his purposes for writing the Gospel, as well as to his use of the genealogy. As a title for the Messiah, Son of David came into Judaism late—not until the first century BC. In *Pss. Sol.* 17.21 the title is used with reference to the political ruler who was to restore the kingdom to Israel. There the author writes: 'Behold, Lord, and raise up for them their king, the son of David...that he may reign over your servant Israel'. Later in the same psalms the author also writes: 'And their king shall be the Messiah of the Lord' (*Pss. Sol.* 17.32). This is the first occurrence in Jewish literature where the term 'Messiah' is applied to a coming ruler from the descendants of David.

The title Son of David occurs in the New Testament only in the Synoptic Gospels. There it is used first in Mark with reference to Jesus as the healer of blind Bartimaeus (Mk 10.46-52; see also Mt. 20.29-34; Lk. 18.35-43). Matthew apparently took over the title Son of David and the idea of healing associated with it from Mark. Matthew then used the combination of ideas to try to persuade his Jewish skeptics that Jesus really was the Messiah. But, as we learn from the incidents reported in Mt. 9.27-34, the Jews were not persuaded. Matthew reports that Jesus healed two blind men who proclaimed him as the 'son of David'. Because of that confession of faith and their expressed belief also that Jesus could heal them, he healed the two men. Then Jesus used reverse psychology by telling the men not to let anyone know what he had done. The psychology worked, because Matthew says, 'But they went away and spread the news about him throughout that district' (Mt. 9.31).

Subsequently, Jesus healed a mute demoniac. After that incident 'the crowds were amazed and said, "Never has anything like this been seen in Israel" '. However, the Pharisees were not convinced and asserted: 'By the ruler of the demons he casts out the demons' (Mt. 9.32-34; see also Mt. 12.22-24).

Also, according to Matthew, Jesus cured blind and lame people in the temple in Jerusalem. Then the children cried out, 'Hosanna to the Son of David'. After that confession of faith, the chief priests and the scribes, also Jewish authorities, 'became angry' (Mt. 21.14-15).

According to Matthew, then, recognizing Jesus as the Son of David was a sign of faith, a faith that his Jewish skeptics did not share. The Pharisees and other Jewish authorities expected the Messiah to be a political figure like the son of David mentioned in the *Psalms of Solomon*, and, indeed, like the one the angel describes to Mary in Lk. 1.31-33: 'He will be great...the Son of the Most High...the throne of his ancestor David...reign over the house of Jacob forever...of his kingdom there will be no end.'

One purpose of Matthew, then, was to try to convince his skeptical fellow Jews, especially their authorities, that Jesus' cures were evidence for believing that he was the messianic Son of David. However, Matthew's purpose for presenting Jesus the Messiah as Son of David in the stories of his birth was not therapeutic, biological or political. It was theological: 'He will save [Greek, *sōzō*] his people from their sins' (Mt. 1.21). 'His people', of course, were Jews like Jesus himself. Thus, according to this statement, Matthew believed that Jesus' saving work was intended for the Jewish people. As we might expect, the same idea is expressed in the psalms quoted above: 'Your love is toward the descendants of Abraham, the children of Israel' (*Pss. Sol.* 18.4).

Apparently, it took Matthew, a Jew converted to the Jesus movement, a while to believe that Jesus' saving work was to be extended to non-Jews. The story that seems to show clearly the change in Matthew's attitude is that of the healing of the Canaanite woman's daughter (Mt. 15.21-28; see also Mk 7.24-30). Now let's see how the dialogue between the woman and Jesus reflects Matthew's own theological beliefs.

The woman approached Jesus about healing her daughter and said, 'Have mercy on me, Lord, Son of David'. At first Jesus ignored her, and his disciples impatiently told him, 'Send her away'. Jesus responded by saying, 'I was sent only to the lost sheep of the house of Israel', that is, the Jews. But kneeling down, the woman said, 'Lord, help me'. Jesus answered, 'It is not fair to take the children's food and throw it to the dogs'. 'Dogs' was a derogatory term used by Jews to refer to Gentiles.

The context of this dialogue indicates that 'the children' are probably to be understood as the Jews, because they thought of themselves as the only children of God. And the food is probably meant to be the message and work of Jesus, including his healings. These sayings of Jesus, then, as reported by Matthew, portray Jesus as wanting to limit his work to his own people, the Jews.

Jesus' statements thus far in the story represent the attitude of Matthew and some other followers of Jesus in his community of believers concerning a mission to Gentiles. They were obviously not in favor of such a mission. And that attitude coincides with Matthew's view stated in his birth stories: Jesus 'will save his people [the Jews] from their sins' (Mt. 1.21).

The story of the Canaanite woman continues. She replies to the coldly negative responses of Jesus to her thus far by saying: 'Yes, Lord, yet even the dogs eat the crumbs that fall from their masters' table'. Finally, Jesus responds positively: 'Woman, great is your faith! Let it be done for you as you wish.' Because of the woman's confession of her faith in Jesus three times as Lord, Jesus grants her wish, and her daughter was healed immediately. It seems, then, that according to Matthew, confession of Jesus as Lord was a basic requirement for admission of Gentiles into the nascent Christian religion. The requirement of faith in Jesus as Lord, along with belief in the resurrection of Jesus, was already present in the teaching of Paul: 'If you confess with your lips that Jesus is Lord and believe...that God raised him from the dead, you will be saved' (Rom. 10.9).

I began the discussion just concluded with Matthew's designation of Jesus as 'son of David'. It represents the view of those followers of Jesus, including Matthew himself when he first believed in Jesus. Jesus' followers maintained that the Christian mission should be limited to Jews. However, Matthew also calls Jesus 'son of Abraham'. Now we want to learn why he probably does so.

Son of Abraham

Jesus' ultimate response to the Canaanite woman as reported by Matthew is meant to serve as instruction concerning a prominent and difficult question in the early church. The question is also reflected in Paul's letters, especially Galatians and Romans, and in the book of Acts: Should the church undertake a mission to Gentiles? And this is where Matthew's Jesus as 'son of Abraham' comes in. Jesus is not only the Jewish Son of David, but he is also 'Son of Abraham' in the sense followers of Jesus came to understand the term. According to that understanding, the descendants of Abraham are no longer limited to Jews. The concept became broadened to include Gentiles who believed in Jesus, and especially those, according to Matthew, who confessed him as Lord. Remember that 'Lord' (*kyrios*) was a title that Gentiles applied to some of their famous men.

In contrast to the title 'son of David', Matthew uses the designation 'son of Abraham' with reference to Jesus only in his first verse. The phrase occurs nowhere else in that way in the New Testament. However, if we take into consideration what Matthew says about Abraham in the body of his Gospel, his use of the title 'son of Abraham' presents a broader picture with regard to Jesus' work of salvation. Salvation is not to be limited to Jews but is also available to Gentiles who have the proper faith, as the story of Jesus healing the Canaanite woman indicates. Matthew believed that as the Son of Abraham Jesus fulfilled God's promise to Abraham: 'In you all the families of the earth shall be blessed' (Gen. 12.3).

The linking together of Jesus to both Abraham and David was present in Christian tradition before Matthew. There is that passage in Rom. 1.3, cited above, where Paul says that Jesus was descended from David. And according to Paul in Gal. 3.6, 'Abraham believed God, and it was reckoned to him as righteousness'. Those who share Abraham's faith are his descendants: 'So, you see, those who believe are the descendants of Abraham' (Gal. 3.7). Paul alludes to Gen. 12.3 or Gen. 18.18 by saying, 'All the Gentiles shall be blessed in you' (i.e. Abraham; Gal. 3.8-9). And in Gal. 3.16 Paul says that the promises to Abraham were made concerning 'one person, who is Christ'.

Matthew later ties the 'son of Abraham' of the genealogy in with the rest of the Gospel very nicely. As we consider Matthew's tie-ins we can better understand why he used the phrase in his preface to the genealogy and what it meant for him. Already in Matthew's story of John the Baptist, the Baptist reportedly says to the Pharisees and Sadducees who came for baptism: 'Do not presume to say to yourselves, "We have Abraham as our ancestor"; for...God is able from these stones to raise up children to Abraham' (Mt. 3.9). This means that Jews should not think they are the only persons who can enter the kingdom of heaven. The point is confirmed in Mt. 8.11, where Matthew reports Jesus as saying: 'Many [i.e. Gentiles] will come from east and west and will eat with Abraham and Isaac and Jacob in the kingdom of heaven'.

According to both Paul and Matthew, the 'descendants of Abraham's family' (Acts 13.26; see also 2 Cor. 11.22; Gal. 3.6-18; Rom. 4.1-16) came to include Gentile as well as Jewish believers. Because Paul and Matthew were Jews who became converts to the Jesus movement, it was only natural that they eventually came to feel as they did. They believed the coming of Jesus made their new conviction possible because Jesus was not only the Son of David but also the Son of Abraham. And that is why Matthew used both phrases as titles for Jesus in the preface to his genealogy of Jesus.

Generations of Jesus' Ancestors

We do not know whether the original author of the Matthean genealogy divided it into three groups of Jesus' ancestors or if Matthew himself did it, but for some reason Matthew says there are 14 generations within each group (Mt. 1.2-6a; 1.6b-11; 1.12-16). However, if you count the generations, you will discover that there are only 13 'fathers' in the first group. In the second group there are 14 fathers, and in the third group there are only 12 fathers, unless we count Joseph as the father of Jesus. Even so, this leaves only 13 fathers. And Matthew, as we have already observed, makes it clear that it is 'Mary, of whom Jesus was born' (Mt. 1.16).

As a tax collector (Mt. 9.9; 10.3) Matthew should have been able to count accurately. But tax collectors in general did not have good reputations for being honest, and sometimes they were thought to be sinful. Zacchaeus 'was a chief tax collector and was rich...one who is a sinner' (Lk. 19.2-10). According to Mt. 9.9-14, after Jesus asked Matthew to follow him, the writer of Matthew links 'tax collectors and sinners' together among those eating with Jesus. Whether Matthew was a sinner, we do not know, yet we might wonder how accurate and honest he had been as a tax collector. It is likely, though, that he really could count accurately and that, therefore, he had some special motive for using the number 14. However, it is more difficult to determine Matthew's motive than to discover that his counting is not accurate. If we assume that Matthew could count accurately, he must have had some reason for ignoring the fact that his numbers did not add up correctly. So here are some suggested explanations for his use of the number 14.

In the Hebrew and Greek alphabets individual letters sometimes represent numerical values, and the letters can be combined to form numbers desired. The three Hebrew consonants in the name David have the numerical equivalent of 14 (*daleth* [4] + *waw* [6] + *daleth* [4] = 14). The difficulty with this view is that only Matthew's Jewish readers would get the point—if that was the point Matthew really wanted to make. There is no way to come up with the same numerical combination for the name David by using the Greek letters for it.

In the Jewish literature of Matthew's time, especially in the apocalypses, writers were fascinated with schemetizing history into periods of 7s and 14s. In *1 En.* 91-93, for example, the writer declares to his sons what had been revealed to him in a heavenly vision. He was born on 'the seventh in the first week'. Then in the remainder of his ten-week span he recounts what will happen in each week with a consistent formula: 'in week so and so such and such will happen'. Of course, a week is seven days, and Matthew's fourteen generations were each made up of seven plus seven, at least theoretically. And Luke probably intended his genealogical list to be thought of in sevens.[5]

The list of generations from Abraham to David ends with the words 'Jesse the father of King David' (Mt. 1.6). The title 'King' does not appear with David in Luke's genealogy, so why may Matthew have added it?

We have learned that Hebrew kings were anointed by a priest or a prophet to rule over the people Israel. This is one of the things that indicate that in Hebrew society religion and political affairs were interrelated. Kings were 'the Lord's anointed' or messiahs. The phrase 'King David' occurs often in the Old Testament, but the esteem associated with David and his descendants was lost after the Exile. By his use of the title 'King' with David, Matthew portrays him as the prototype of Jesus. And 'Jesus the Messiah, the son of David' (Mt. 1.1) becomes the one expected to revive the Davidic esteem when the kingdom the Jews hoped for comes. (Read here again the passage in Lk. 1.31-33 quoted above.) According to Acts 1.6, Jesus' first followers had expected him to 'restore the kingdom to Israel'. Matthew writes that Jesus 'was born king of the Jews' (Mt. 2.2; see also Mt. 21.5). For Matthew, then, the title 'King' with David has religious-political significance not only for David but also for Jesus. The writer of the Gospel of John reports that Jesus was recognized as 'the King of Israel' during his public career (Jn 1.49; see also 12.13-15).

As the first Jewish followers of Jesus developed christological beliefs about him, the genealogies were an obvious and necessary attempt to convince other Jews that their Messiah Jesus was truly of Davidic descent. There is no record that Jesus himself ever claimed such descent. As a matter of fact, in one incident in the Synoptic Gospels Jesus is presented as not interested in making such a claim. Indeed, Jesus is portrayed as if he were making another claim for himself, the title 'Lord': 'While Jesus was teaching in the temple, he said, "How can the scribes

5. See especially Goulder, *Luke*, I, pp. 281-90.

say that the Messiah is the son of David? David himself, by the Holy Spirit, declared, 'The Lord said to my Lord' [a quotation from Ps. 110.1, thought to be written by David]... David himself calls him Lord, so how can he be his son?"' (Mk 12.35-37; see also Mt. 22.41-45; Lk. 20.41-44).

It seems plausible to believe that the genealogies of Jesus were composed after his death but before belief in the virgin birth had become widely accepted. The genealogies that appear in Matthew and Luke are probably based on earlier lists, as has been suggested. The belief in Jesus as the Son of God was not known to the original writer of the Lukan genealogy. For reasons we shall learn later, Luke concludes his account of the genealogy with the words 'son of Adam, son of God' (Lk. 3.38). Indeed, in the bodies of both the Gospel of Matthew and of Luke the people of Jesus' hometown did not know about the extraordinary circumstances of his birth and infancy. They knew Jesus as 'the carpenter, the son of Mary' (Mk 6.3), 'the carpenter's son' (Mt. 13.55) or as 'Joseph's son' (Lk. 4.22).

Later I shall have more to say about the differences between the two genealogies. But now I turn to a significant and interesting difference from Luke in Matthew's genealogy.

Chapter 2

MATTHEW'S WOMEN IN THE GENEALOGY OF JESUS

In both the Gospel and Acts Luke has a special concern for women. Besides Elizabeth, Mary and the prophetess Anna in the birth stories, elsewhere Luke mentions the widow (7.11-17), the woman sinner (7.36-50), the women with Jesus (8.1-3), Mary and Martha (10.38-42), a woman in the crowd (11.27-28), the crippled woman (13.10-17) and the woman with the coins (15.8-10; see also Acts 1.14; 5.1-11; 9.36-41; 12.12-17; 13.50; 16.13-15; 17.4, 12). With the exception of Mary and Martha (see Jn 11.1–12.3), the women mentioned appear only in Luke's Gospel.

In light of Luke's special interest in women both in his Gospel and in Acts, we might expect to find the names of several in his genealogy, but he does not even include the name of Mary. On the other hand, the names of four women, in addition to Mary, appear in Matthew's genealogy (Mt. 1.5-6). We may suspect, therefore, that Matthew has inserted the names of the women in an earlier genealogical list of men. That is why in the title of this chapter I have written 'Matthew's Women in the Genealogy of Jesus' instead of 'The Women in Matthew's Genealogy of Jesus'.

If the names of the women were in a common core of original material, why would Luke, so interested in women elsewhere, have omitted them? And if Matthew inserted the names, why did he choose them over such universally recognized pious Jewish women as Sarah, Rebekah, Rachel and Leah?

The Women in the Old Testament

There is not an outstanding example of moral integrity among the women Matthew mentions. Tamar, Canaanite wife of Judah's son Er, disguised herself as a prostitute in order to seduce her father-in-law Judah, so that she could bear a child (Gen. 38). Rahab was a professional prostitute in ancient Jericho who hid the Israelite spies sent there by Joshua on the roof of her house under some stalks of flax. In return, the Israelites spared her life when they later captured the city (Josh. 2.1-25). Ruth, a Moabite girl, showed admirable conduct in that she loved and remained loyal to her mother-in-law, a Hebrew woman. But Ruth lost her virtue one night after a party during the grain festival when she lifted the cover off the legs of Boaz and slept with him.[1] He later became her husband (Ruth 3). The fourth woman (Bathsheba), the wife of Uriah the Hittite, took a bath in just the right season—'the spring of the year'—and the right place to be seen by David as he was strolling on the roof of the palace. She later became pregnant by David, who then had her husband Uriah killed in battle to make his marriage to her easier (2 Sam. 11–12).

Why Did Matthew Insert the Names of Those Women?

Why would Matthew ever include the names of such disreputable women in a genealogy of Jesus the Messiah? Elsewhere[2] I have defended the view that Matthew included the names of the women to counter a Jewish accusation that Jesus was the illegitimate son of Mary. Here some of the evidence for my view is repeated, with much new material added, because I still think it is the most likely explanation for Matthew's insertion of the names of the four women. Otherwise, why would he not have inserted the names of Sarah, Rebekah, Rachel and Leah, women universally recognized by Jews as virtuous? One would expect to see them in a list that included the virgin Mary.

Jewish Accusation of Illegitimacy

Throughout his Gospel Matthew reflects a Christian polemic against the Jews or a polemic of the Christian church against the Jewish synagogue. Within the controversy between Jews and Christians there was the Jewish accusation that Jesus was the illegitimate son of Mary. Such an

1. The Hebrew text of Ruth 3 is somewhat ambiguous, with words of double meanings and sexual implications. On these points, discussed in a nontechnical way, see E.F. Campbell, Jr, *Ruth* (AB, 7; Garden City, NY: Doubleday, 1975), pp. 116-38.

2. Edwin D. Freed, 'The Women in Matthew's Genealogy', *JSNT* 29 (1987), pp. 3-19. For the view expressed here and for other views see Brown, *Birth*, pp. 71-74, and especially J. Schaberg, *The Illegitimacy of Jesus* (San Francisco: Harper & Row, 1987). Schaberg opts for the illegitimacy of Jesus.

accusation can be documented from both Jewish and Christian writings of the second century and later. It is impossible to tell, though, whether the charges in this literature stem from Jewish sources independent of the Gospels or are based on certain passages in the Gospels that could be considered as evidence for illegitimacy.

Evidence in the New Testament. Several phenomena in the Gospels already reflect grounds for accusations of illegitimacy or misconduct on Mary's part.

1. *Absence and Silence of Joseph.* It is curious that although Joseph plays a prominent part in Matthew's stories of Jesus' birth, he never appears with Mary. He is conspicuously absent when the wise men pay their worshipful respects to the baby Jesus. Matthew writes: 'On entering the house, they saw the child with Mary his mother' (Mt. 2.11). Yet, after the wise men left, an angel told Joseph to take the child and his mother and flee to Egypt (Mt. 2.13). Joseph's absence in the scene with the wise men in Matthew is in sharp contrast to the Lukan scene of the shepherds: 'So they went with haste and found Mary and Joseph, and the child lying in the manger' (Lk. 2.16).

In Matthew's story of Jesus' birth both Mary and Joseph are portrayed as silent characters; neither person ever says a word. Joseph never speaks anywhere else in either Matthew or Luke. And there is no public appearance of Joseph reported anywhere except in Luke's stories, where he does appear with Mary on several occasions. Mary accompanies Joseph to Bethlehem for the registration (Lk. 2.4-7). Both parents take the baby Jesus up to Jerusalem to present him to the Lord in accordance with the Jewish law. While they are there, Jesus' 'father and mother were amazed at what was being said about him' (Lk. 2.22-38). After they had fulfilled their obligation to the law, they returned to Galilee (Lk. 2.39-40). And when Jesus was 12 years old, his parents took him along to Jerusalem for the festival of the Passover (Lk. 2.41-51).

In contrast to the silent Mary in Matthew's account, Mary does speak, sometimes prominently, in Luke's narrative. She speaks to the angel (Lk. 1.34, 38). She speaks or sings the Magnificat (Lk. 1.46-55), and she scolds Jesus for not staying with her and his father in the crowds in Jerusalem during the Passover festival (Lk. 2.48).

With the exception of Luke, Joseph is not mentioned by name anywhere in the Synoptic Gospels (see Jn 1.45; 6.42). In the story of Jesus' rejection at Nazareth Mark reports that the people of Nazareth ask, 'Is not this the carpenter, the son of Mary?' (Mk 6.3). Matthew reports the people of Nazareth, Jesus' hometown, as asking, 'Is not this the carpenter's son? Is not his mother called Mary?' (Mt. 13.55). And Luke reads, 'Is not this Joseph's son?' (Lk. 4.22). With Matthew and Luke, especially the latter, we should compare Jn 6.42: 'Is not this Jesus, the son of Joseph, whose father and mother we know?' Consider also Jn 1.45, where Philip says to Nathanael, 'We have found him about whom Moses...wrote, Jesus son of Joseph from Nazareth'.

Mark's complete silence concerning Joseph might mean that Jesus did not have a human father and, therefore, could indicate Mark's awareness of the story of the virgin. If that was the case, then the tradition of Jesus as 'Joseph's son' (Lk. 4.22) would have developed later than the tradition of the virgin birth, of which Luke seems to have been aware. But that seems unlikely, especially if the virgin birth had become a part of Christian faith. Or, since Joseph does not appear in person in the body of any Gospel, Mark's silence could imply that Joseph had died before Jesus became a public figure. Or, the silence of Mark, especially when considered with the designation 'son of Mary' (see below), could be construed as a scornful remark signifying the illegitimacy of Jesus.

2. *Mary in the Gospels.* Jews customarily referred to a man as the son of his father, not of his mother, whether or not the father was still living. Jesus is called the son of Joseph in Lk. 3.23; 4.22; Jn 1.45; and Jn 6.42. Insofar as I know, the only exception to the rule of paternity in the Old Testament is Judg. 11.1: 'Jephthah...the son of a prostitute, was a mighty warrior'. Was Jephthah referred to as the son of his mother and not of his father because his mother was a prostitute? In the passage quoted above Matthew changed the reading of Mark—'Is not this the carpenter, the son of Mary?'—to 'Is not this the carpenter's son?' Did Matthew do that because he realized the insinuation of illegitimacy in the Markan phrase, 'the son of Mary'? Luke's reading, 'Joseph's son', is in harmony with his understanding of the paternity of Jesus elsewhere, including the stories of Jesus' birth.

Another incident, according to Mark, that may reflect the accusation of illegitimacy is the disrespectful attitude of Jesus not only toward his brothers and sisters but toward his mother as well. When Jesus' mother and brothers came seeking him and the crowd reported to Jesus that they were asking for him, Jesus responded, 'Who are my mother and my brothers?' and 'Here are my mother and my brothers. Whoever does the will of God is my brother and sister and mother' (Mk 3.31-35). Notice that 'father' is omitted, and it is also omitted in the parallel accounts (Mt. 12.46-50; Lk. 8.19-21). Why is 'father' not included? Think about possible answers to that question.

There may be an even more uncomplimentary remark of Jesus about his mother reported in Lk. 11.27-28. Jesus made a statement about an unclean spirit going out of a person and returning to cause a worse state of the person. Then an admiring woman in the crowd remarked, 'Blessed is the womb that bore you and the breasts that nursed you!' Jesus' response again is negative: 'Blessed rather are those who hear the word of God and obey it!'[3]

Notice that this blessing by Jesus stands in sharp contrast to Luke's statements in his birth stories. There Elizabeth exclaims about Mary, 'Blessed are you among women, and blessed is the fruit of your womb' (Lk. 1.42; see also 1.45). Jesus' response even contradicts the words Luke puts on Mary's lips in her Magnificat: 'Surely, from now on all generations will call me blessed' (Lk. 1.48). This blessing echoes Leah's statement at the birth of her son Asher: 'Blessed am I, because all the women will bless me' (LXX Gen. 30.13).

The saying of the woman blessing Jesus is only in Luke's Gospel. Since Jesus' response contradicts what Luke says with respect to Mary in his birth stories, it may be an actual saying of Jesus. Luke would, then, have felt the need to report it because it is a genuine saying. At the same time, Jesus' negative response to the woman would be an unwitting indication on Luke's part of the Jewish charge of illegitimacy.

Two statements in John 8 throw further light on the matter under discussion. There the questions of who is the real father of the Jews and of Jesus and of illegitimacy are the main concerns. In Jn 8.19 the Jews reply to a statement of Jesus about God as his Father by asking, 'Where is your Father?' The Jews claim descent from their father Abraham, and later they say, '*We* are not illegitimate children; *we* have one father, God himself' (Jn 8.41; my emphasis). If the emphatic 'we', present in the Greek text, implies that Jesus is illegitimate but that his Jewish critics are not, then the implications are clear. Since John was written during a time of intense controversy with the Jews, it is very likely that the

3. As is to be expected, there are differences of opinion about the degree of negativity in Jesus' response. For further study see Fitzmyer, *Gospel*, II, pp. 926-29; I.H. Marshall, *The Gospel of Luke* (Grand Rapids: Eerdmans, 1978), p. 482.

passages in John 8 reflect the Jewish accusation of illegitimacy.

What Matthew says in Mt. 1.18-20 may well have been taken by Jewish adversaries of Jesus' followers as indicating the illegitimacy of Jesus. Matthew writes: 'When his [Jesus'] mother Mary had been engaged to Joseph, but before they lived together, she was found to be with child from the Holy Spirit'. The response of Joseph—who, Matthew says, was 'a righteous man'—to the situation only gave support for the Jewish view. Joseph did not want to 'expose' Mary 'to public disgrace' and 'planned to dismiss her quietly' (Mt. 1.19). But, interestingly enough, at just the right moment, before Joseph could carry out his plan to dismiss Mary, an angel of the Lord appeared to him in a dream. The angel persuaded Joseph to change his own plan and follow God's plan: 'Take Mary as your wife, for the child conceived in her is from the Holy Spirit' (Mt. 1.20). As we shall learn later, Matthew uses 'a dream' as a literary device to move his narrative along and to give reasons why things happen as they do.

Matthew may well have used the genealogy of Jesus and composed the rest of the narrative in Mt. 1.18-25 to reply to the Jewish accusation of illegitimacy. It was precisely the pregnancy of Mary that had to be defended. Matthew states his defense of Mary in three chief ways. First, he inserts the names of the four notorious women into an earlier genealogy, which probably did not have them. Second, he uses the Greek, instead of the Hebrew, text of Isa. 7.14 (see discussions of this passage below) to show the prophecy of a virginal conception. And third, he has Joseph accept (take) Mary as his wife and name her son.

Thus, Matthew tries to refute the Jewish accusation of the illegitimacy of Jesus in a manner prospective Jewish converts to whom he was writing could understand and, hopefully, accept. Matthew justifies the behavior of Mary in the same way Jews came to justify—even extol—the conduct of the four women mentioned in the genealogy (see below). Mary is included with those four women, then, not as an immoral person but as a paragon of virtue. Why? Because she gave birth to the Messiah. In 1.18 Matthew begins his story of Jesus' birth by saying: 'Now the birth of Jesus the Messiah took place in this way'.

We have learned that the four women were not shining lights of moral probity when judged by the standards in the Hebrew scriptures. The spontaneous reaction of devout Jews of Jesus' time to the conduct of the women, with the possible exception of Ruth, would have been very unfavorable. However, by the time Matthew wrote his Gospel

Jewish rabbinic scholars were beginning to think of those women no longer as sinners. By the rabbis they were defended as distinguished, even righteous, women in Jewish history because each had done something notable for the Jewish people. Below are some examples of how Matthew's women are portrayed in some Jewish literature after Old Testament times.

The Women in Rabbinic Literature

The legends that developed around the women listed in Matthew's genealogy are extensive. So the following are only several of many taken from the Talmud and Midrash, collections of teachings and interpretations of scriptures by rabbis after New Testament times. In general, the women are excused of any guilt, and the men involved with them are portrayed as placing the blame upon themselves.

Tamar

Before you begin to read this section please read the story of Tamar in Gen. 38.6-26 in the Old Testament, and compare it with what is said here.

'Tamar knew that she was appointed to be the ancestress of David and of the Messiah, and she determined...to make sure of fulfilling her destiny. Accordingly, when the holy spirit revealed to her that Judah was going up to Timnah', she prepared to meet him. When Judah passed by her, she prayed to God that she should not 'go forth empty from the house of this pious man'. When Tamar learned that she was pregnant, she 'felt very happy and proud, for she knew that she would be the mother of kings and redeemers'. But when her condition became known, she was forcibly dragged before the court, liable to death by burning, the penalty for 'a high priest's daughter that leads an unchaste life' (see Lev. 21.9). Tamar prayed for God's grace, and God sent the angel Michael to help her. Judah acknowledged his sin and declared the innocence of Tamar, and then a heavenly voice said, 'ye are both innocent!' Tamar afterward became a convert to the Hebrew religion.[4]

In this Jewish legend the behavior of Tamar was motivated by the Holy Spirit, and it was primarily responsible for her pregnancy. Notice here the similarity in the story of Matthew who twice mentions that

4. Lewis Ginzberg, *The Legends of the Jews* (7 vols.; Philadelphia: Jewish Publication Society of America, 1959–68), II, pp. 34-36.

Mary's pregnancy was 'from the Holy Spirit' (Mt. 1.18, 20). And, as with Joseph, who is called 'a righteous man' in Matthew's story, Judah is described as 'this pious man'.

According to another legend, as in the story about Joseph (Mt. 1.20-24), an angel from God persuaded Judah to change his mind, although not for exactly the same reason that Joseph changed his mind. Judah decided to have intercourse with Tamar instead of continuing on his way. Joseph, who had no sexual relations with Mary, 'planned to dismiss her quietly' after he learned that she was 'with child from the Holy Spirit' (Mt. 1.18-19). In the rabbinic story the Holy Spirit exclaimed: 'Through Me...did these things occur' (*Gen. R.* 85.12). A statement about the Holy Spirit is a characteristic feature of most legends about the four women, as with Mary.

Rahab

Please read now the story about Rahab in Josh. 2.1-24. Many Jewish legends developed concerning Rahab, because 'There was no prince or ruler who had not possessed Rahab the Harlot'. She was a prostitute during the 40 years the Israelites spent in the desert. At the age of 50 she became a convert to Judaism. 'Said she: "May I be forgiven as a reward for the cord, window and flax" ' (*Zeb.* 116ab; see Josh. 2.6, 18, 21).

Rahab lived an immoral life for 40 years, but when Israel moved into Canaan, she worshiped the true God, lived as a pious convert, and, as Joshua's wife, 'became the ancestress of eight prophets and of the prophetess Huldah'.[5]

It was said, 'the Holy One, blessed be He, looks out for a righteous person among the peoples of the world, as, e.g., Jethro, Rahab, Ruth' (*Eccl. R.* 5.11). Rahab saved two lives for God, and God saved many lives because of her. If there had been 200 men in her family and 200 families connected with them, they would all have been saved through Rahab's merit (*Eccl. R.* 5.6).

Rabbis taught that there were four women of surpassing beauty in the world: Sarah, Rahab, Abigail and Esther (*Meg.* 15a). Some rabbis said that the divine spirit rested upon Rahab before Israel entered Canaan. If the divine spirit had not rested upon her, she would not have known that those pursuing Joshua would return in three days (*Ruth R.* 2.1).

5. Ginzberg, *Legends*, IV, p. 5.

Ruth

Please read ch. 3 in the Old Testament book of Ruth. Ruth, the great-grandmother of David, was an ancestress of the Messiah even though a Moabite, not a Hebrew woman. Rabbinic tradition has it that she was destined for that role by God's plan. Kings and prophets were to spring from her uterus because of the good she had done for her mother-in-law. The statement of Ruth to Naomi in Ruth 1.16, 'Your people shall be my people, and your God my God', showed her determination to become a convert to the Hebrew religion.

An angel led Ruth to the field of Boaz, who 'admired her for her grace, her decorous conduct, her modest demeanor'. She was so extraordinarily beautiful that she was afraid to walk alone at night because men could not see her without falling passionately in love with her. As with Bathsheba, Ruth was listed among the most pious women; and like Rahab and Bathsheba, Ruth was among the 22 'women of valor'.[6]

The six measures of barley that Boaz gave to Ruth (Ruth 3.15-17) indicated that 'she was destined to become the ancestress of six pious men who would be endowed with six spiritual gifts'. Among the men were David, Daniel and the Messiah. Under the power of the Holy Spirit, Boaz had intimated to Ruth that the royal house of David was destined to come forth from her (*Šab.* 113b). Although Ruth was 40 years old, Naomi called her 'my daughter'. The reason was that although Ruth was 40, she looked like a girl of 14 (*Ruth R.* 4.4).

According to the Jewish legend, Ruth was very modest: All the other women bend down to gather the ears of corn, but she sits and gathers; all the other women hitch up their skirts, and she keeps hers down; all the other women jest with the reapers, while she is reserved (*Ruth R.* 4.6).

Boaz, called 'this righteous man', made an oath: 'As the Lord liveth I shall not touch this woman to-night!' (*Num. R.* 15.16). All that night Boaz lay stretched out upon his face, and prayed, 'Lord of the Universe, it is revealed and known to Thee that I did not touch her; so may it be Thy will that it be not known that the woman came to the threshing-floor, that the name of Heaven be not profaned through me' (*Ruth R.* 7.1).

As with Joseph in Matthew's story and Judah in the rabbinic story about Tamar, Boaz is called a 'righteous man'. The writer is careful to say that Boaz did not have sexual relations with his girlfriend Ruth. In

6. Ginzberg, *Legends*, V, p. 258.

the same way, according to Matthew, Joseph 'had no marital relations with her [Mary, his girlfriend] until she had borne a son' (Mt. 1.25).

The legends about Ruth do protest too much. Rabbis overly stress that Boaz did not touch Ruth on the threshing floor, obviously to counteract the euphemisms for sexual relations in the Hebrew text of Ruth. In this way the virtue of Ruth is preserved.

Wife of Uriah (Bathsheba)

The interesting story of David and Bathsheba is recorded in 2 Samuel 11–12. Please read those chapters now.

David became the number one hero in Jewish lore, and his wife Bathsheba also came to be venerated. According to rabbinic legend, she had been destined by God from the creation of the world to become David's wife, but he took her while she was not mature. The rabbis figured out mathematically that Bathsheba was only six years of age when she conceived. The rabbis' mathematics must have been worse than Matthew's.

As with Rahab and Ruth, Bathsheba was regarded as one of the 22 'women of valor', as well as one of the 22 'women of virtue', who are praised in Proverbs 31. Through the Holy Spirit she had foreseen that her son Solomon would be the wisest of men.[7]

When Bathsheba was told that Solomon was spending too much time in bed with his Egyptian bride, Bathsheba rebuked him by saying, 'Thy father...was known to all as a God-fearing man, and now people will say, "Solomon is the son of Bathsheba, it is his mother's fault if he goes wrong"'.[8] (Recall 'son of Mary' in Mark and our discussion of that phrase above.) According to the rabbinic legend, the murder David committed and his adultery were excused because of extenuating circumstances. Since in David's time it was customary for soldiers to give their wives bills of divorce, and since Uriah was killed in battle, Bathsheba was free to marry.[9]

The Women in Contemporary Jewish Writings

Much of the material with respect to Matthew's four women in the genealogy of Jesus presented thus far comes from sources later than the

7. Ginzberg, *Legends*, V, p. 258.
8. Ginzberg, *Legends*, IV, p. 129.
9. Ginzberg, *Legends*, IV, p. 103.

Gospels. However, there are some of the same ideas in contemporary Jewish and Christian writings.

Testaments of the Twelve Patriarchs

In the *Testaments of the Twelve Patriarchs* (c. 140 BC–AD 100) the author overdoes the guilt of Judah and stresses the innocence of Tamar in several ways. He omits the reference in Gen. 38.24 to Tamar as having 'played the whore' and to her pregnancy 'as a result of whoredom'. Tamar's behavior is explained or excused as customary: 'For it was a law of the Amorites that a woman who was a widow should sit in prostitution seven days by the gate' of the city. If the Amorites, a Semitic people who preceded the Hebrews in parts of the ancient world, had a law like that, I am not aware of it.

There is another element added in the *Testaments of the Twelve Patriarchs* that is not in Genesis. When Judah heard that Tamar had conceived, he wanted to have her burned, but he found out who she was. That much of the story is in Genesis 38, but the writer of the *Testaments of the Twelve Patriarchs* adds: 'I could not kill her because it [Tamar's pregnancy] was from the Lord'. Here, as in the Talmud and Midrash, Tamar acted in accordance with God's will (*T. Jud.* 10.1–12.12).

As with Mary, Tamar became pregnant because it was the will of God.

Philo of Alexandria

In the writings of Philo, Jewish philosopher and allegorist who wrote in Greek (c. 20 BC–AD 30), Tamar is portrayed as a symbol of virtue, even chastity. Typically, Philo writes allegorically that Tamar was a widow—but not for the reason we might think. She was widowed not because she lost her husband, but because she lost the passions that corrupt the mind:

> She has left for ever the intercourse and society of mortals and remained...widowed of human pleasures. Thus she receives the divine impregnation, and, being filled with the seeds of virtue, bears them in her womb and is in travail with noble actions (*Deus Imm.* 29 [136-37]).

According to Philo, virtue, when she does not find zeal and earnestness among her scholars,

> veils her face and sits like Tamar at the cross-roads, presenting the appearance of a harlot... Her wish is that inquiring minds may unveil and reveal her and gaze upon the glorious beauty, inviolate, undefiled and truly virginal, of her modesty and chastity (*Congr.* 23 [124]).

Philo's words 'truly virginal' stress that condition for Tamar, just as it is stressed for Mary in Matthew's story. In his discussion of divine parenthood, Philo illustrates his point with Tamar, who 'bore within her womb the divine seed, but had not seen the sower [God, the one responsible for her pregnancy]. For we are told that...she veiled her face' (Gen. 38.14-15). Philo says that the pledges given by Judah all belong to God, so Tamar as virtue or soul is, at least by implication, made pregnant by God (*Mut. Nom.* 23 [134-36]; see also *Fug.* 27 [149]).

In *Virt.* 40 [220-22] Philo says that Tamar was from Syria, a land full of many gods and idols, but that she risked her life to join 'the camp of piety'. Although she married two wicked men, 'she...kept her own life stainless and was able to win the good report which belongs to the good and to become the original source to which the nobility of all who followed her can be traced'.

These passages show that by the time of Jesus in at least some Jewish circles Tamar was not regarded as one who had committed an immoral act. Rather, she was considered a paragon of virtue. Her behavior, including her pregnancy, had come to be regarded as initiated by God, exactly as in Matthew's story about Mary.

Josephus

The treatment of Rahab, the prostitute, by Josephus is also interesting, especially because of the way he leaves out some objectionable details and changes others. In *Ant.* 5.1.2 he does not mention the word 'prostitute', which is used in Josh. 2.1. Instead, Josephus uses 'innkeeper' and refers to Rahab's house as an 'inn' (Greek, *katagōgion*; Luke's word for 'inn' is *katalyma* in Lk. 2.7, discussed below).

There are other curious changes in Josephus's retelling of the story of the Israelite spies, Rahab and Joshua. In Josh. 2.9 it is reported that Rahab knew that the Lord had given the Israelites the land of Canaan, had delivered them at the Red Sea, and made them victorious over their enemies. She is made to acknowledge: 'The Lord your God is indeed God in heaven above and on earth below' (Josh. 2.8-11). But how she learned these things is not stated. Josephus, however, says that God himself revealed them directly to Rahab: 'For of this (she said) she knew through certain signs which God had given her' (*Ant.* 5.1.2). This is an important difference because it shows that, according to Josephus, God's plan was behind Rahab's actions.

The narratives in Josh. 2.8-25 and 6.22-25 give the impression that Rahab was unmarried, because her family mentioned are father, mother, brothers and sisters. Josephus, on the other hand, does not mention her father's family, father, mother, brothers or sisters. Josephus, therefore, is writing about Rahab and her own family, not the family of her father and mother. He speaks about 'the inn of Rahab', 'her household' and 'her family'. None of these expressions occurs in the account of Rahab in the Septuagint. The word translated as 'family' is *genea*, the usual word for 'offspring' (*Ant.* 5.1.3). So the traditions that Rahab had progeny and that she was a woman worthy of respect are at least as old as the time of Josephus and, so, also of the time of Matthew and Luke. Josephus closes his story about Joshua and Rahab by saying: 'Indeed he presented her with lands forthwith and showed her every consideration', that is, honor and respect (*Ant.* 5.1.7).

In the treatment of David, Bathsheba and Uriah, Josephus seems to stand in between the account in the Old Testament and that in later Jewish writings. As in the Old Testament story, Bathsheba is 'very beautiful', but Josephus adds 'and surpassed all other women' (*Ant.* 7.7.1). According to 2 Sam. 11.5, when Bathsheba realized she was pregnant, 'she sent and told David, "I am pregnant" '. That is all she says. However, Josephus expands the account and writes that Bathsheba 'sent to the king, asking him to contrive some way of concealing her sin—for, according to the laws of the fathers, she was deserving of death as an adulteress' (*Ant.* 7.7.1).

Josephus's account of Bathsheba's request and his comment about Jewish law are expansions of the Old Testament narrative and reflect the usual Old Testament view that Bathsheba's conduct was immoral. Joseph's wanting to dismiss Mary quietly after realizing she was pregnant reflects the same view. Josephus's words, 'asking him to contrive some way of concealing her sin', seem to anticipate the later view of some rabbis that Bathsheba was not guilty of adultery.

Josephus's account of David and Uriah is much amplified. David orders his general Joab to 'punish Uriah, whom he made out to be a guilty man'. Here again Josephus seems to anticipate the later rabbinic view that Uriah deserved to die because he did not obey the king's command to go home to his wife after returning from battle. We cannot say that Josephus actually intended to make either David or Bathsheba innocent of wrongdoing. But it seems as though he took a giant step toward that end, an end clearly achieved in later Jewish writings.

In the case of Ruth, however, Josephus leaves no doubt about her innocence, as well as the innocence of Boaz. By leaving out a detail or two and by adding other details, Josephus makes it clear that, although Ruth had spent a night sleeping with Boaz, the pair had done nothing wrong. Josephus omits the part about Ruth uncovering the legs of Boaz (Ruth 3.7) and other Hebrew expressions in Ruth 3 that have clear sexual implications.

Both the Old Testament and Josephus report that when Boaz woke up to find a woman lying with him, he asked who she was. In Ruth 3.9 Ruth replies, 'I am Ruth, your servant; spread your cloak over your servant, for you are next-of-kin'. Boaz responds by asking a blessing for her from the Lord and says that her last kindness is better than the first, because she had not gone after young men, rich or poor.

Josephus says that in reply to the question about who she was Ruth 'mentioned her name and prayed him, as her master, to pardon her' and that Boaz 'held his peace'. The writer in Ruth 3.14-16 continues by saying that Ruth lay at the feet of Boaz 'until morning, but got up before one person could recognize another; for he said, "It must not be known that the woman came to the threshing floor" '. Then Boaz gave Ruth some barley and sent her back to her mother-in-law. Josephus's version, continuing after the words 'held his peace', reads:

> but at daybreak, before his servants began to move to work, he aroused her and bade her take as much of the barley as she could carry and go to her mother-in-law, before anyone should see that she had slept there, since it was wise to guard against scandal of that kind, and the more so when nothing had happened (*Ant*. 5.9.3).

In this passage Josephus's view is made quite clear. Although Ruth and Boaz spent the night lying together, they did not have sexual intercourse, as the words 'nothing had passed' indicate. Josephus's stress on Ruth's innocence seems as though it was, indeed, written to counter the implications of sexual misconduct on the part of Ruth implied in the Old Testament text.

The story of Ruth, both in the Old Testament and Josephus, ends with the marriage of Boaz and Ruth and the birth of their son Obed, who became the father of Jesse, who became the father of David. Ruth 4.13 reads: 'So Boaz took Ruth and she became his wife. When they came together, the Lord made her conceive, and she bore a son.' Josephus adds a detail of time: 'Boaz married Ruth, and a year after a boy was born to them' (*Ant*. 5.9.4). The implication of Josephus's words is clear: Ruth had not become pregnant before she was married. This is in strong contrast to Mary, who had become pregnant before Joseph took her as his wife. One might wonder how Josephus would have dealt with Matthew's story of Mary's conception, were he to have written about it.

The Women in Contemporary Christian Writings

By the end of the first century AD, in three different Christian circles, Rahab was regarded in one way or another as an example of the way to salvation.

1 Clement

According to the author of this work, which was probably written sometime between AD 75–120, 'Rahab the prostitute was saved because of her faith and hospitality'. The scarlet thread that she hung from her house was a clear sign that 'for all who believe and hope in God there will be redemption through the blood of the Lord'. Rahab was an example 'not only of faith but also of prophecy' (*1 Clem.* 12.7-8).

Hebrews

For the author of Hebrews, written about the same time as *1 Clement*, Rahab ranks among a number of Old Testament characters cited as examples of faith: 'By faith Rahab the prostitute did not perish with those who were disobedient, because she had received the spies in peace' (Heb. 11.31).

James

The author of James writes that 'Rahab the prostitute' was 'justified by works when she welcomed the messengers and sent them out by another road' (*Jas* 2.25). Recall that in the Talmudic tractate *Zeb.* 116a the spies are also called messengers. The statement of James that Rahab sent them off in another direction is intended to reinforce her good work.

Although the writer of each of these Christian works refers to Rahab as a prostitute, as does the Old Testament, she is made a model of faith or of action on behalf of the Hebrew people to be admired, even imitated.

Matthew's Defense against the Jewish Accusation of Illegitimacy

Matthew inserts the names of the four women—Tamar, Rahab, Ruth and the wife of Uriah (Bathsheba)—into the genealogy that he had somehow obtained. The behavior of those women was such that initially

they would not have merited a place among the ancestors of the Messiah. Mary's conception before marriage, even during the period of betrothal, would have been considered immoral by most Jews. Matthew defends the behavior of Mary in a manner he hoped would assuage his Jewish adversaries whom he wanted to persuade that Jesus was the Messiah.

With all of the women it was thought that God or the Holy Spirit intervened in their lives. The divine action took place not only in the relationships of the women and the men associated with them. By divine power the women's lives were also transformed from those of questionable, if not sinful, natures to states of innocence or virtue. In accordance with such views, Matthew uses the examples of the women as a defense against the Jewish accusation. But there is more to Matthew's defense tactics.

Role of Joseph

In Matthew's polemic with the Jews, Joseph, not Mary, plays the key role. He represents both the initial Jewish reaction to Mary's pregnancy by wanting to dismiss (divorce) her and the desired Christian acceptance by later taking her for his wife. In only eight verses (Mt. 1.18-25) Matthew writes four times about the conception of Jesus without male participation. However, he does not emphasize the miracle of conception but focuses attention on how Joseph reacts. His first reaction is to 'dismiss her quietly' so as not 'to expose her to public disgrace'. The statement that Joseph was 'a righteous man' reflects the usual Jewish sensitivity toward the observance of the law with respect to sexual relations.

In Old Testament law the penalty for the rape of an engaged virgin was death. If a man has sexual relations with such a woman in the town where she lives, both shall be stoned to death, 'the young woman because she did not cry for help in the town and the man because he violated his neighbor's wife'. But if the woman is raped in the open country, where a cry for help would not be heard, only the man is to be put to death (Deut. 22.23-27). If a man rapes a virgin who is not engaged, and they are caught in the act, the man shall pay a fee to the woman's father, and she shall become his wife. And because he raped the woman, he would not be permitted to divorce her as long as he lived.

It is clear that Joseph had not raped Mary, so according to Jewish law, he did not have to marry her. At the same time, he would have been permitted to divorce her because he was not married to her. We should learn here that Matthew's word *apoluō*, translated as 'dismiss' in the NRSV, may also be translated as 'divorce'. It is translated that way in the NRSV at Mt. 5.31-32; Mk 10.2, 4, 11; Lk. 16.18; and other places.

In Jewish society the line between betrothal and marriage was a fine one. Evidence in the Old Testament is ambiguous, to say the least. Two passages are sometimes alleged to indicate that betrothal and marriage were the same thing except for the formal marriage ceremony, if any. According to 2 Sam. 3.14, 'David sent messengers to Saul's son Ish-baal, saying: "Give me my wife Michal, to whom I became engaged" '. This passage seems to indicate that a woman was considered the wife of the person to whom she had become engaged. But the argument is useless historically because in 1 Sam. 18.20-27 we learn that Saul gave David 'his daughter Michal as a wife' in return for the marriage present of 100 Philistine foreskins that Saul had requested, because he thought David would be killed in battle with the Philistines. In this passage there is no reference to an engagement or sexual relations. Yet, if Matthew was aware of the passage in 2 Sam. 3.14, it would help to explain his words about Mary being engaged to Joseph and about Joseph being told to take her as his wife. However, Joseph does not ask that Mary be given to him as his wife, nor does he mention anything about being engaged to her.

According to Gen. 19.12-14, some men living with Lot are referred to as 'sons-in-law, who were to marry his daughters'. This is the NRSV translation, and as such, it could be taken to imply that since the men are called sons-in-law, they were living as married and, therefore, presumably having sexual relations with Lot's daughters to whom they were engaged. However, the Hebrew verb translated as 'were to marry' (future) could also, perhaps better, be taken as past action—'had married'—as in the Septuagint. Perhaps because of the difficulty with the text, the REB omits the words that the sons-in-law 'were to marry his daughters' (engagement?).

According to later Jewish custom, marriages were arranged beforehand. They were initiated by the father of the man and agreed to by the father of the woman involved. Persons who planned to be married were expected to have a formal betrothal (*shiddukkin*). However, such a betrothal did not establish any marital relationship (but see Lk. 1.5: 'Mary, to whom he was engaged and who was expecting a child').

Moreover, both the woman and the man were free to break the agreement. Eventually there was a marriage contract (*ketubah*) signed by two male witnesses not related to either party concerned or to each other. A bill of divorce (*get*) was required for breaking either a betrothal or marriage contract.

The idea of a formal paper of betrothal may help to explain why Joseph and Mary had no sexual relations as engaged persons. Perhaps they did not have the formal *shiddukkin*. The requirement of a paper of divorce (*get*) for breaking an engagement may help to explain Joseph's plan to divorce (a good translation of Matthew's word *apoluō*; so Brown[10]) Mary quietly and the reference to her as his wife. As 'a righteous man', obedient to the Jewish law, Joseph was embarrassed by Mary's wrongdoing. At the same time, Joseph's plans do nothing to establish the innocence of Mary. And just when Joseph had decided to divorce Mary, an angel of the Lord appeared to him in a dream to interrupt his plans, because the Lord had a plan for him. As with some of Matthew's four notorious/famous women, who had already had a part in God's plan, Mary was the instrument of God, through the Holy Spirit, in giving birth to the Messiah.

Quotation from Isaiah 7.14

In order to help convince his Jewish critics with respect to Mary's behavior, Matthew interrupts his story of Mary and Joseph by quoting from Isa. 7.14. The quotation interrupts the thought sequence between Mt. 1.21 and 1.24. By leaving out vv. 22 and 23 the thought in v. 24 follows smoothly after v. 21. Moreover, in each of the other dreams of Joseph (Mt. 2.13-15 and 2.19-23) Joseph's response to the dream comes immediately after the angel has finished speaking to him. And in each of the dream episodes the citation of an Old Testament passage being fulfilled comes at the end and does not interrupt the flow of thought in the narrative, as it does in Mt. 1.22-23.

Matthew inserts the quotation in its present place because he wants to end the story about Mary's conception precisely as he does. She fulfilled a prophecy of God that a virgin would conceive and give birth to a special child. In order to do this Matthew chooses the Greek text 'the virgin' of Isa. 7.14 over the Hebrew, 'the young woman'. Moreover, in giving birth to Jesus Mary had not, as Matthew's Jewish adversaries

10. Brown, *Birth*, pp. 122, 128.

were contending, acted immorally. Why? Because, as with the four women, the Holy Spirit was really responsible for her manner of life.

Joseph's Acceptance of Mary

Matthew's last tactic in his defense against the Jewish accusation of the illegitimacy of Jesus is to have Joseph take Mary as his wife and name her son. Matthew ends his genealogy not with the statement 'Joseph the father [lit. 'begot'] of Jesus', as with every other ancestor, but with the words 'Joseph the husband of Mary, of whom Jesus was born' (Mt. 1.16). As a descendant of Mary but not of Joseph Jesus could not have been in the lineage of David. Again, Joseph, who is addressed as 'son of David' by the angel (Mt. 1.20), is given the key role in the story. He accepts Mary as his wife and names her son, as the angel had instructed him: 'You are to name him Jesus' (Mt. 1.21). Joseph later gave him that name: 'And he named him Jesus' (Mt. 1.25).

Far too much weight has been given to the naming of Jesus by Joseph.[11] There is no direct evidence for the naming of a Jewish child in the first century. In the Old Testament fathers name sons (Gen. 5.3, 29; 1 Chron. 7.23; so Matthew; cf. Lk. 2.21), but so do mothers (Gen. 4.25; 29.32-33; 1 Sam. 1.20; 4.21; see Lk. 1.31). In fact, there are more times in the Old Testament when a mother names a son than when a father does.

There were no public witnesses to the naming of Jesus as there were to the naming of John (Lk. 1.57-63). Matthew, however, did not report the naming of Jesus for the information of the public but for the purpose of convincing his critics who were questioning the legitimacy of Jesus' birth, and thus also his messiahship. Joseph's acceptance of Mary helped to make her legitimately the one 'of whom Jesus was born, who is called the Messiah' (Mt. 1.16). Thus, Matthew is not only concerned with showing, in his confused way, Jesus' Davidic heritage but also with vindicating Mary from Jewish accusations. But let us consider the matter further.

According to Brown, Matthew thought 'that by accepting the child as his own Joseph gives Jesus a Davidic genealogy'. The emphasis must be on what Matthew thought. In my opinion such a situation would be unlikely in real Jewish life, and Brown gives no evidence for it. Moreover, Joseph actually accepted Mary, not the child. Brown also says that

11. Brown, *Birth*, pp. 130, 132, 139.

by naming the child Joseph becomes Jesus' legal father and cites *B. Bat.* 8.6 as evidence: 'If a man said, "This is my son", he may be believed'.[12] It is interesting to recall here God's words at the baptism of Jesus: 'This is my Son' (Mt. 3.17; see also Mk 1.11; Lk. 3.22), the same words as those in the Mishnah. Should we not expect Matthew to have used a similar formula in reporting Joseph's acceptance of Jesus as his son? Joseph never says of Jesus, 'This is my son'.

The purpose of the more formalized statement in the Mishnah was to free a widow of the levirate law. According to the law of 'levirate marriage' (Hebrew, *levir*, 'brother-in-law'), if a brother 'dies and has no son, the wife of the deceased shall not be married outside the family to a stranger. Her husband's brother shall go in to her, taking her in marriage, and performing the duty of a husband's brother to her' (Deut. 25.5-10). The purpose of the law, of course, was to preserve the name of the deceased brother. There is nothing to indicate that this is what Matthew had in mind.

From some ancient Near Eastern texts we learn that adoption was practiced by several Semitic peoples. However, there is no law of adoption in the Old Testament, in spite of certain passages that are sometimes taken as reflecting the practice. For Judaism in Palestine after the Exile there is no certain evidence whatsoever for adoption. Nor is adoption known as a legal practice in rabbinic Judaism. Although rabbinic law does provide instances similar to those existing in legal adoptions, there is no case like that of Joseph and Mary reported by Matthew. The closest thing pertaining to it is the rabbinic rule: 'Scripture looks upon one who brings up an orphan as if he had begotten him' (*Sanh.* 19b). Although Matthew was hardly aware of the rabbinic rule, did he think of Jesus as an orphan because he had no human father and therefore have Joseph provide him fatherly care? Joseph seems to have been the natural choice since he had been engaged to Mary.

Although there is no evidence that Joseph adopted Jesus, rabbinic law did not forbid the 'adoptive' father from calling the one 'adopted' his son or the 'adopted' son from calling the adopter his father.[13] However, Matthew nowhere refers to Joseph as Jesus' father and conspicuously avoids doing so at the end of his genealogy in Mt. 1.16. This is

12. Brown, *Birth*, pp. 132, 139.

13. The information for the preceding discussion is taken from 'Adoption', in *EncJud*, II, pp. 298-303.

in strong contrast to Luke who regularly refers to Joseph as Jesus' father, as we shall learn in more detail later.

There is no evidence either for the naming of a child in the first century AD or for the legalizing of children—if that is what Matthew and some of his interpreters have in mind. And even if Joseph did adopt Mary's son and give him a name, this would not place Jesus in Joseph's lineage as a descendant of David.

Because there are no indications of formal adoption or of legality in Matthew's story of the naming of Jesus, we should make nothing of it. After all, by naming Mary's son Joseph was only doing what the angel had told him to do. The Greek name *'ēsous* is the same as the Hebrew 'Joshua' or *Yehoshuah* and means 'Yahweh is salvation', 'Yahweh saves' or Yahweh will save'. Obviously, Matthew found this to his liking, so for him the name was purely symbolic: 'He will save his people from their sins' (Mt. 1.20-21).

As we know from Josephus, who mentions many men with that name, the name 'Jesus' in its Hebrew form 'Joshua' was very common among Jews of the first century AD. But for Gentiles the name would have no significant meaning, so Matthew was apparently writing for unbelieving Jews. The point is not in the naming of Jesus but in having Joseph take ('accept') Mary with him as his wife. That was Joseph's key role in Matthew's story.

In sum, Matthew uses three main tactics in his defense against the Jewish accusation of the illegitimacy of Jesus. First, he inserts into the genealogy the names of the four women, notorious characters in the Old Testament. However, by Matthew's time in some circles they had come to be regarded as virtuous because each had done something for the Hebrew people. Second, Matthew chooses the Greek text of Isa. 7.14 ('the virgin') over the Hebrew text ('the young woman') and uses the quotation, along with the angel's statement about the action of the Holy Spirit, in order to justify the behavior of Mary, as with that of the four women. In this way Matthew confirms Mary in her role in begetting the Messiah. And third, he has Joseph take Mary as his wife and name Jesus as directed by the angel in order to show his acceptance not only of Mary and her son but especially his acceptance of God's will. For Matthew the point is in Joseph's acceptance of Mary, not as the mother of an illegitimate son, as perceived by his critics, but as a virtuous woman, whose pregnancy was the will of God in order to give birth to the Messiah.

What Did Matthew Himself Believe?

Finally, we should raise the question of whether or not Matthew himself shared the view of his Jewish critics about the illegitimacy of Jesus. If he did, he could still write to defend it because of his Christian beliefs about Jesus. If he shared the view of illegitimacy, he could also share the view of some Jews that, as with the other women in his genealogy, Mary was virtuous because, in her case, she actually gave birth to the Messiah through the power of the Holy Spirit. She would no longer be regarded as a notorious woman but as a notable one.

On the other hand, there are at least two main reasons for thinking that Matthew believed the story of Jesus' birth from a virgin, again because of his Christian beliefs about Jesus. First, if he did not believe in such a birth, he probably would not have reported it and, therefore, would have felt no need to defend it. Second, instead of quoting the Hebrew text of Isa. 7.14, which reads 'the young woman', he uses the Greek text, which reads 'the virgin', as evidence from prophecy for his belief.

Having stated his reasons for the legitimate birth of Jesus, Matthew turns to some reactions to that birth. But before I consider them I want to observe further some of the differences between the stories of Jesus' birth as told by Matthew and Luke.

Chapter 3

Comparisons between the Stories of Matthew and Luke

The Genealogies

Basic sources used in the original compositions of the genealogies in Matthew and Luke are the Old Testament narratives of the kings of Judah in 1 and 2 Kings, as well as the genealogies listed in 1 and 2 Chronicles and Ruth 4.18-22. There are, however, many deviations, intentional or unintentional, from the Old Testament accounts both in Matthew and Luke. Because there are so many differences in the genealogies, most scholars maintain that they were composed independently. But recall the view of Goulder that Luke structured his birth narratives, including the genealogy, on the basis of Mark's germ of the idea and especially Matthew's account.

It is impossible to tell to what extent each writer used the Old Testament and other material that was at hand from earlier Christian traditions. And, as we shall see, there are good reasons to believe that each writer created much of the material himself, a point too often understressed, it seems to me.

More Differences between the Genealogies

There is a vast difference in the purposes of the genealogies of the Old Testament and those of the New Testament. In the Old Testament the common purpose of the writers was to trace a special person's descendants from a common ancestor. The purpose of the Matthean and Lukan genealogies, on the other hand, was to trace the lineage of Jesus through David from whom the Messiah was to be descended. However, in the process, there are remarkable differences in how each writer gets to David.

Matthew (1.2-16) and Luke (3.23-38) give the genealogies in reverse order. Matthew begins with Abraham and comes down the lineage through David to Joseph, husband of Mary. Luke (3.23-38), on the other hand, begins with Joseph, the father of Jesus, and traces the lineage backward through David to Adam, son of God.

Except for differences in the forms of one or two names, both writers agree on the names between Abraham and David. But from David to Joseph Matthew lists 25 names in the family tree; Luke has 40 (according to the standard Nestle Greek text). However, they agree on only two names: Zerubbabel and his father Shealtiel. Observe that in Lk. 3.36 the name Cainan is repeated in the next verse and that there are different relatives on each side of the name: 'Shelah, son of Cainan, son of Arphaxad... Mahalaleel, son of Cainan, son of Enos'. There is even no similarity among the names. Incidentally, the number of total names in the genealogies is not the same in several of the important manuscripts of the New Testament. In Luke, for example, the number varies from 72 to 78.[1]

Anyone fascinated with names and numbers should be sure to consider carefully Goulder's ingenious discussion of Luke's genealogy.[2] Taking his clue from contemporary literature, especially apocalypses, where there is a 'schematizing of history into sevens and fourteens', he finds 11 sevens of names in Luke's genealogy. Not only the numbers are important, but Luke has invented individual names 'for symbolic reasons'. 'So', according to Goulder, 'the genealogy looks like a carefully constructed work of art, a genealogical poem'.

With respect to the relationship between the two genealogies, according to Goulder, Luke knew the one of Matthew, who was also creative, in his own way. Luke 'wanted to follow the same idea on a larger scale, and to a more ambitious plan'. For Goulder, therefore, the genealogy is in no way historical, so he differs from Brown,[3] who finds some historical value in the genealogies.

Another rather obvious difference between the two genealogies (especially in the Greek text) is the terminology used. Matthew uses the verb *gennaō*, meaning 'beget' or 'procreate as the father'. The NRSV and the REB translate it as 'was the father of'. Luke, on the other hand, uses the name followed by the genitive of the article, *'Iōsēph tou 'Eli* ('Joseph the [son of] Heli'). Whereas Matthew uses qualifying words and phrases, for example, 'the king' after the name David (Greek text) and 'to the deportation to Babylon', Luke does not use such qualifiers. Nor

1. See Fitzmyer, *Gospel*, I, pp. 490-97.
2. Goulder, *Luke*, I, pp. 283-91.
3. Brown, *Birth*, pp. 87-94 and Appendix 2, pp. 505-12.

does Luke divide the genealogy into three sections with 14 generations in each.

Jesus and the Jewish Expectation of Two Messiahs

As with Matthew, Luke certainly used the genealogy to show that Jesus was in the lineage of David and that therefore he had the proper lineage to qualify as Messiah. However, in Lk. 1.5 Luke writes that Elizabeth 'was a descendant of Aaron' and in 1.36 that Elizabeth was a relative of Mary. This seems to indicate that Mary was not in the line of David but, as with Elizabeth, in the lineage of Aaron. It may be, though, that Luke wanted to have it both ways, as the following observations seem to indicate.

As a descendant of David, the Messiah was expected to be a royal figure who would restore the kingly rule to Israel. Although there was a diversity of opinions about the Messiah and his coming, this was probably the most widely accepted messianic belief. However, some Jews expected the coming of two Messiahs: one from the line of David and the other from the line of Aaron. We know this from the Qumran Scrolls and other Jewish literature. Writers from Qumran speak of 'the Messiah of Aaron and of Israel' (1QS 9.11; 1QSa 2.11-21; see CD 12.23; 14.19; 19.10).

The writer of *T. Reub.* 6.8-12 speaks of the 'Messiah High Priest' from Levi and of a king from Judah 'chosen to reign over all the nations...an eternal king'. Compare Lk. 1.33: 'He [Jesus] will reign over the house of Jacob forever, and of his kingdom there will be no end'. According to *T. Sim.* 7.2, 'The Lord will raise up someone from Levi as high priest and someone from Judah as a king (God and man). He will save all the Gentiles and the tribe of Israel.' Compare Lk. 2.29-32: 'Your salvation, which you have prepared in the presence of all peoples, a light for revelation to the Gentiles and for glory to your people Israel'. The Messiah of Aaron was to be the high priest and first in rank. The Messiah of Israel was to be the political leader and was subordinate in rank to the priestly Messiah.

One might question whether Luke wanted to say that as a descendant of David on Joseph's side of the family and of Aaron on Mary's side of the family, Jesus possessed all the qualifications required for the Messiah as Priest/King.

The genealogies raise problems for which there are no completely satisfactory solutions. How conscious would the humble couple from

Nazareth have been of their ancestral line? In sum, the one historical element in the genealogies is that they indicate there was a time in the formation of Gospel traditions when Jesus was simply regarded as the natural-born son of Joseph and Mary. Why? Because only through Joseph could the lineage of Jesus as the Messiah be traced back to David.

The First Two Words of Matthew's Gospel

The first two words of Matthew's Gospel (*biblos geneseōs*), translated as 'An account of the genealogy' in the NRSV, have occasioned a wide difference of opinion among scholars about their meaning and purpose. Most scholars agree that the words are to be taken as the title for at least Mt. 1.1-17. According to N.J. Nolland,[4] other scholars have 'over-interpreted' Matthew's first two words in an effort to gain new insight into his theology. Nolland maintains that the word *genesis* is a heading for only Mt. 1.1-17, not for the whole book. Matthew 1.18-25 is, then, 'an explanatory supplement'.

But did Matthew intend the first two words of his Gospel to be the title for something more than Mt. 1.1-17? Are they to serve as a title for all of ch. 1 or for the first two chapters or for a longer section of the Gospel, as, for example, Mt. 1.1–4.16? Or did Matthew intend his opening words to be applied to the whole Gospel? Accordingly, the words, which literally mean 'book of (a or the) beginning', have been taken to mean either record, book or account of the history of the birth, origins, genealogy, generations or life of Jesus the Messiah (Christ).

Matthew's expression *biblos geneseōs* seems to show influence from the Septuagint of Genesis—a point denied by Nolland—where the phrase occurs in Gen. 2.4 and 5.1. Matthew is closer to Gen. 5.1, which reads: 'This is the book of the beginning of human beings' (*hautē hē biblos geneseōs anthrōpōn*). In the verses that follow the writer gives the descendants of Adam.

The Greek word *biblos* may also be translated as 'roll' or 'scroll'. Perhaps it should be taken that way in LXX Gen. 5.1: 'This is the scroll [roll] of the beginning of human beings'. The Hebrew word translated as *biblos* in the Septuagint means 'record' or, as in the NRSV, 'list'. Perhaps on the basis of Gen. 5.1 we should take Matthew's first four words

4. N.J. Nolland, 'What Kind of Genesis Do We Have in Matt 1.1?', *NTS* 42 (1996), pp. 463-71.

as meaning, 'the record (list) of the ancestors of Jesus Christ'. If so, the words would apply only to the genealogy in Mt. 1.1-16.

In the Old Testament, genealogies are used to introduce and show the significance of some unusual person. Surely, the original genealogies of Jesus, no matter by whom they were written, were intended to do the same thing. Genesis 5.28 introduces the story of Noah and Gen. 11.26, the story of Abraham. It is probably not coincidental that Matthew calls Joseph 'a righteous man' just as in Gen. 6.9 Noah is called 'a righteous man, blameless'. Abraham was told by God, 'Be righteous' (Gen. 17.1). Luke says of Zechariah and Elizabeth, 'Both of them were righteous before God' (Lk. 1.6).

Although we cannot be sure how much of the Gospel Matthew meant to include under his first two words, the word *genesis* ties the genealogy of Jesus in with the story of his birth that follows in Mt. 1.18-25. In Mt. 1.18, then, the word *genesis* should be translated as 'birth', as also in Lk. 1.14. Should we, therefore, translate Mt. 1.1 as 'An account of the birth [so the NRSV in a footnote] of Jesus the Messiah'? If so, Matthew's words would apply at least to Mt. 1.1-25. The REB limits the meaning: 'The genealogy of Jesus Christ'. So much for Matthew's first two words.

Comparison of the Stories of Jesus' Birth as a Whole

Matthew 1–2	*Luke 1–2*
1. Gospel begins with genealogy of Jesus	Gospel begins with formal preface; genealogy in ch. 3
2. Jesus a descendant of David	Jesus a descendant of David
3. Mary engaged to Joseph	Mary engaged to Joseph
4. Couple had no sexual intercourse	Couple had no sexual intercourse
5. Joseph, husband of Mary	Mary does not know a man
6. Mary, wife of Joseph	Joseph, father of Jesus
7. Joseph a descendant of David	Joseph a descendant of David
8. Holy Spirit responsible for conception of Jesus	Holy Spirit responsible for conception of Jesus
9. Unnamed angel tells Joseph of coming birth	Angel Gabriel tells Mary of coming birth

	Matthew 1–2	*Luke 1–2*
10.	Angel tells Joseph, 'You are to name him Jesus'	Gabriel tells Mary, 'You will name him Jesus'
11.	Jesus 'will save his people from their sins'	Jesus is 'a Savior, who is the Messiah, the Lord'
12.	Joseph and Mary may have lived together before birth of Jesus	Joseph and Mary may have lived together before birth of Jesus
13.	Old Testament prophecy implies Mary is a virgin	Mary called a virgin
14.	Joseph and Mary live in Bethlehem	Joseph and Mary go to Bethlehem from Nazareth to be registered
15.	Jesus born in Bethlehem, perhaps in a house (Mt. 2.11)	Jesus born and laid in a manger in Bethlehem
16.	Birth in Bethlehem fulfills Old Testament prophecy	Birth in Bethlehem takes place while there for registration
17.		Birth of John promised by Gabriel to father Zechariah
18.		Mary visits Elizabeth, mother of John
19.		Birth of John
20.		Poetic passages based on various sources, including Old Testament
21.	Visit of wise men to house in Bethlehem	Visit of shepherds to manger in Bethlehem
22.	Visitors had been informed of Jesus' birth in supernatural manner	Visitors had been informed of Jesus' birth in supernatural manner
23.	Visitors return from whence they came	Visitors return from whence they came
24.	Flight to Egypt and Herod's murder of children fulfill Old Testament prophecies	
25.		Simeon predicts a sword will pierce the soul of Mary
26.		Circumcision of Jesus, presentation of Jesus in temple and purification of Mary

	Matthew 1–2	*Luke 1–2*
27.		Joseph and Mary referred to as parents of Jesus and as father and mother of Jesus
28.		Mary herself refers to Joseph as father of Jesus
29.	Joseph and family return to Judea from Egypt which fulfills Old Testament prophecy	
30.	Joseph and family go to Nazareth to live, which fulfills Old Testament prophecy	Joseph and family return from Bethlehem to Nazareth, 'their own town', to live
31.	Herod, king of Judea	Herod, king of Judea
32.	Archelaus, son of Herod, succeeds his father	
33.		Augustus, emperor of Rome
34.		Quirinius, governor of Syria
35.		Jesus in temple in Jerusalem at twelve years of age

There is essential agreement on 16 points (2, 3, 4, 7, 8, 9, 10, 11, 12, 13, 15, 21, 22, 23, 30, 31). Even in the other items there are common elements that are treated somewhat differently by each author. The similarities may mean that Matthew and Luke each used a core of traditional material, the usual view. The differences suggest that each writer added materials from other sources and/or incorporated some material of his own creation. If we consider these things, along with the differences in literary style, method and theological interests of the authors, the least we can say is that Matthew and Luke each adapted the material, of whatever origin, to conform to his purposes for writing. And, in most cases, each author wrote in his characteristic literary style. Creativity on the part of each writer should not be understressed. I shall discuss these topics later.

The Conception of Jesus According to Matthew

I have discussed the relationship of Joseph and Mary as engaged persons and, at the same time, also as man and wife. I have proposed that Matthew composed the story of Jesus' conception in response to the

Jewish accusation of the illegitimacy of Jesus. The main point is that Mary's conduct was regarded as somehow wrong by Joseph, who plays the key role in Matthew's story and who represents the Jewish public. The translations bring out this point, yet it is frequently neglected in the commentaries. Any misgiving on the part of Joseph toward Mary is entirely absent from Luke's story.

Some things in Matthew's story of the conception of Jesus are very personal matters, especially the part about sexual relations. And that makes it more difficult for us to understand the actual relationship between Joseph and Mary. We must understand that in Matthew's time Jews did not talk about sex as freely as persons do today. So how did the one telling the story in the first place learn about these personal matters? Did Mary or Joseph speak publicly about them? Did they keep a diary that somehow got into the hands of a zealous storyteller? If we think about these things seriously, perhaps the best answer to the questions, after all, is that the stories really are the creations of the writers themselves. Luke's story, though, does not raise the same problems.

The Conception of Jesus According to Luke

In contrast to Matthew, where an angel appears to Joseph, in Luke (1.26-38) God sends the angel Gabriel to Mary, 'a virgin engaged to a man whose name was Joseph'. The angel tells Mary that she is a 'favored one' and 'The Lord is with you'. Recall the meaning of the name Emmanuel, 'God is with us' (Mt. 1.23). Mary is perplexed and wonders what the greeting means. Then the angel says, 'Do not be afraid, Mary'.

In ancient literature fear is a common motif in accounts of supernatural visions. The literary accounts of Jesus' birth are no exceptions. Fear on the part of persons having visions and the response of the angels, 'Do not be afraid', are regular refrains in the stories of Jesus' birth, especially in Luke. For Joseph see Mt. 1.20; for Zechariah, Lk. 1.12-13; for Mary, Lk. 1.29-30; and for the shepherds, Lk. 2.9-10. And the fear is always followed by a message of good news (see also Acts 18.9; 27.21-26).

Goulder makes a strong case, in my opinion, for Matthew's story as the source of Luke's. Indeed, 'Luke is rewriting Mt. 1'. But, according to Goulder, Luke is writing something more important without denying the truth of what Matthew says. Matthew was 'a conventional Jewish male chauvinist' who thought of 'the putative father' in relating his story of Jesus' birth. For Luke 'women were in many ways the spiritual equals of men'. He had known women such as Lydia, Damaris and Priscilla, leaders in their respective churches. Mary was among those waiting the arrival of the Holy Spirit (Acts 1.12-15). It was only fitting that Luke neglect Joseph and has an annunciation to Mary. Matthew had named four mothers in Hebrew history, 'perhaps as four notable instances of God's transcending the normal ways of marriage'. But these women, as we have learned, were originally regarded as notorious, not notable. It may be, though, that because Luke knew the women of Matthew he recounts, according to Goulder, 'the fulfillment of different mothers in Israel, especially Sarah and Hannah'.[5] On the other hand, I believe it could be precisely because Luke knew Matthew's women, in spite of his own special interest in Mary and other women, that he did not mention Matthew's women. He did not have to use the names of the women as examples in order to defend Mary against the charge of illegitimacy. Why? Because for Luke Joseph was the father of Jesus, and Mary and Joseph were his 'parents' (see below).

The angel assures Mary that she has God's favor and says about the child in her womb, 'You will name him Jesus. He will be great, and will be called the Son of the Most High, and the Lord God will give to him the throne of his ancestor David. He will reign over the house of Jacob forever, and of his kingdom there will be no end' (Lk. 1.32-33). Here there are ideas not mentioned in Matthew with reference to Jesus.

The words in Luke are curious, indeed, found in the Gospel of a non-Jewish writer. One might, rather, expect to find them in Matthew, written by a Jew, because they reflect the typical Jewish ideas of a royal Messiah to come (see, e.g., Isa. 9.6-7; Dan 7.13-14).

Did Luke use a Jewish Christian's story of Jesus' birth like that of Matthew or one unlike that used by Matthew? Or, as a scholar of the Septuagint, did Luke himself compose the story of the angel and Mary from passages in the Septuagint? Compare the angel's message to Mary with the prophet Nathan's message from the Lord to David: 'I will make for you a great name... I will establish the throne of his kingdom forever. I will be a father to him, and he shall be a son to me... Your house and your kingdom shall be made sure forever.'

There are surprisingly similar words and ideas similar to those in Lk. 1.32-33 in the messianic hymn in *T. Levi* 18.3-4, 7-8:

5. Goulder, *Luke*, I, p. 227.

> His star shall arise in heaven as of a king... And he shall be magnified in the world... And there shall be peace in all the earth [see Lk. 2.14]... And the glory of the Most High shall be uttered over him... And no one shall succeed him for all generations forever.

There are both words and ideas in other Jewish literature like those of Luke. Consider carefully the following passages from the *Psalms of Solomon* 17 and 18, and observe how many parallels in thought and language there are with Luke's stories of Jesus' birth.

> We hope in God our savior... Lord, you chose David to be king over Israel, and swore to him about his descendants forever, that his kingdom should not fail before you... See, Lord, and raise up for them their king, the son of David, to rule over your servant Israel... Undergird him with...strength...in wisdom... And he will have gentile nations serving him...and he will glorify the Lord...nations to come from the ends of the earth to see his glory...and to see the glory of the Lord... And he will be a righteous king over them...and their king shall be the Lord Messiah... Nor will he build up hope in a multitude for a day of war...for God made him powerful in the holy spirit and wise in the counsel of understanding, with strength... He will lead them all in holiness...and your love is for the descendants of Abraham... Your discipline for us (is) as (for) a first-born son, an only child...for the appointed day when his Messiah will reign.[6]

Although Mary surely was not aware of such lofty messianic ideas, the angel, according to Luke, had told her enough about the coming Messiah Jesus to make her question the angel, 'How can this be, since I am a virgin?' (Lk. 1.34).

Sexual Relations of Joseph and Mary

The Greek text of Lk. 1.34 is literally: 'How is this possible, since I do not know a man?' The word *ginōskō* usually means 'know' in the sense of 'acquire knowledge', 'learn', 'understand' or 'comprehend'. When used with persons, it can also mean 'know someone'. It has that meaning in both the Septuagint and the New Testament. 'The ox knows its owner, and the ass the crib of its master, but Israel does not know me' (LXX Isa. 1.3). 'How can I obtain the money from him, since he does not know me and I do not know him?' (Tob. 5.2; see also Tob. 7.4).

6. *Pss. Sol.* 17.3-4, 22-23, 30-33, 37, 41; 18.3-5. Translation by R.B. Wright, in *OTP*, II, pp. 665-69.

Nathanael asked Jesus, 'Where did you get to know me?' (Jn 1.48; see also Jn 2.24; 10.14-15; Acts 19.15).

Ginōskō is also used by ancient writers as a euphemism for sexual relations. It is used that way in the Septuagint, where it translates a comparable Hebrew word, with reference to both women and men. For men see, for example, Gen. 4.1: 'Now the man knew his wife Eve, and she conceived and bore Cain' (see also 1 Sam. 1.19). For women see LXX Judg. 11.39, where we read that the daughter of Jephthah 'did not know a man' (see also LXX Judg. 21.12). *Ginōskō* is clearly used with the sexual meaning in Mt. 1.25: Joseph 'had no marital relations with [did not know] her until she had borne a son'. Here the meaning is not the least bit ambiguous, in contrast to its use in Lk. 1.34, where the meaning certainly is ambiguous.

Luke has no statement comparable to the one in Mt. 1.25 about Joseph not having sexual relations with Mary until after she had given birth to a son. Does this mean that if we read Luke without first having read Matthew, we would not know of Mary's conception while still a virgin? Does this mean also that as a virgin Mary's first sexual intercourse was with Joseph and that she then conceived in the normal manner? Indeed, this is very likely in light of Luke's statement in Lk. 2.5 that 'Joseph went to be registered with Mary, to whom he was engaged and who was expecting a child'. Is it not strange that in this context there is not even a hint about the miraculous conception of Jesus mentioned in Lk. 1.26-38?

I suggest that because of Luke's special interest in historical reporting he composed 2.1-7 before 1.26-38—that what he says is not always accurate (see below) is beside the point here. The two verses about Jesus' birth (Lk. 2.6-7) correspond to the two about the birth of John (Lk. 1.57-58). Although it is impossible to be sure of the chronological sequence in which the various parts of Luke's stories were written, I suspect that Luke wrote 1.26-38 after he learned about the miraculous conception of Jesus either from Matthew or, possibly, from some source not known to us. And after the tradition of Mary the virgin became known, the words 'as was thought' were added to Luke's genealogy of Jesus.

One reason for believing that Luke himself did not add those words is that he consistently thinks of Jesus as Joseph's son. Indeed, this would be the natural assumption if we had only Luke's story in Lk. 2.1-7 and his genealogy of Jesus without the added words 'as was thought', which certainly were not a part of his original genealogy. If we think of things in this way, there is nothing in Luke's account in Lk. 1.23-38 to preclude a natural conception of Jesus through Joseph.

Surely, Luke could still think of Jesus as the Son of God, although conceived in the normal way but made possible by the power of the Holy Spirit. All this is, indeed, plausible if we read Lk. 1.26-38 with our minds closed to Matthew's story of the virgin Mary. At any rate, unlike Matthew, Luke never leaves any question about the paternity of Jesus elsewhere. So, apparently he was not a member of social or religious circles where the illegitimacy of Jesus and the virginal conception were matters for discussion.

The view that an independent reading of Luke with respect to the virginity of Mary would leave one thinking the conception of Jesus happened in the normal manner was proposed by J.A. Fitzmyer.[7] Brown's view, in agreement with that of most scholars, is that Luke '*does* intend a virginal conception'. Brown's setting off the parallelism between the announcement of John's birth and that of Jesus' birth, along with the power of the Spirit coming upon Mary, has convinced Fitzmyer that there is 'a more extraordinary conception, hence, virginal'. The step-parallelism shows the superiority of Jesus over John and would 'fail completely', according to Brown, if John 'was conceived in an extraordinary manner and Jesus in a natural manner'.[8]

My response is as follows. Luke wrote both the accounts of an annunciation to Zechariah and the one to Mary. What he writes throughout shows the superiority of Jesus over John. The conception of Elizabeth by the power of God ('the angel of the Lord'; Lk. 1.11) is no more miraculous than the conception of Sarah or Hannah. God said to Abraham about Sarah, 'I will give you a son by her' (Gen. 17.15-16). God granted the petition of Hannah for a male child (1 Sam. 1.9-20). The conception of Elizabeth through the Spirit in Luke is not unique, and he may have gotten the idea from Matthew: 'The child conceived in her is from the Holy Spirit' (Mt. 1.20). We have learned that a belief in the power of the Spirit active in the lives of women who were or became virtuous through the Spirit was a rather common phenomenon in Jewish literature.

7. 'The Virginal Conception of Jesus in the New Testament', *TS* 34 (1973), pp. 541-75.

8. See Brown, *Birth*, pp. 299-301 and Fitzmyer, *Gospel*, I, p. 338.

With respect to the conception of Jesus, the superiority of Jesus over John is due to the operation of the Spirit in bringing it about. John will be 'filled with the Holy Spirit even from his mother's womb' (Lk. 1.15; Brown's translation).[9] 'From his mother's womb' is a Hebrew expression and means 'from birth' as in Judg. 13.5, 7; 16.17; Isa. 48.8; and Ps. 22.10-11, translated that way in the Septuagint, NRSV and REB. I have not found an Old Testament passage to confirm Brown's view that the Lukan expression should be taken as 'the time when the child is still in the womb'. Brown thinks that meaning is confirmed by Lk. 1.44, Elizabeth's child leaping in her own womb. But the child in Mary's womb did not leap.

The NRSV translation of Lk. 1.15, 'even before his birth', is very misleading and is inconsistent with its translations of the Old Testament passages cited above. The REB has the meaning precisely correct: 'From his very birth he will be filled with the Holy Spirit'.

Even if we accept Brown's interpretation, Jesus is still superior to John, because even Jesus' conception was the result of the Holy Spirit coming upon Mary. Remember that, according to Luke, as with Matthew (1.18), Mary was already engaged to Joseph. Luke says nothing about the Holy Spirit coming upon Elizabeth. However, the Holy Spirit's action could have taken place through the normal sexual relations between Joseph and Mary, could it not? Luke's emphasis is on the power of the Holy Spirit, not on the virginity of Mary. The Holy Spirit is a special interest of Luke's, as we shall learn.

The Spirit 'coming upon' is a unique feature of Luke's literary style (see below). And there is nothing in Luke comparable to 'the virgin shall conceive' in Matthew. I think Fitzmyer's original view is still the correct one, at least as considered thus far.

It appears, then, that the respective stories of the conception were created by their authors, each in his own way and for his own reasons. Thus, they have absolutely no historical significance. We should, however, consider a related matter, one that at first may seem insignificant but actually may be very important.

The word *anēr* in Lk. 1.34, Mary's reply to the angel, can mean either 'man' (as in a footnote in the NRSV) or 'husband'. See Mt. 1.19: 'her husband ['man'] Joseph'. *Anēr* is the counterpart to *gynē*, meaning

9. Brown, *Birth*, pp. 256, 261.

either 'woman' or 'wife' (see Mt. 1.20, 24; Lk. 1.5, 13, 24). So, then, the interpreter is faced with the question of how to translate the Greek words *ginōskō* and *anēr* in Lk. 1.34.

Mary's words can be taken as meaning 'I do not know a husband' or 'I do not have sexual intercourse with a husband'. Mary's words could also mean 'I do not have a man in my life' or 'I am not intimately acquainted with a male companion'. If we take the words that way, the meaning contradicts the words of Lk. 1.27, 'engaged to a man [*anēr*] whose name was Joseph' (see also Lk. 2.5). If we take Mary's statement to mean 'I do not have sexual relations with a man', it could imply Mary is still a virgin. However, the translation 'I am a virgin' (NRSV and REB) has little basis in the immediate context of her words. On the other hand, the Greek text could mean that Mary is not presently having sexual relations with any man.

However, if Mary's words are taken to mean virginity as, for example, in LXX Judg. 11.39 (*hautē ouk egnō andra*; 'she did not know a man'), then Luke's explanation of her becoming pregnant by the power of the Holy Spirit could be taken as a defense against the Jewish accusation of illegitimacy. If her words are taken as an innocent confession of not knowing a man intimately, they are a contradiction of being engaged to Joseph and pregnant. This seems to make the first alternative preferable because it coincides with Matthew's defense of Mary with the explanation of her conception as the fulfillment of the prophecy about the virgin in Isa. 7.14. Thus, Luke would unwittingly, along with Matthew, be using Mary's pregnancy as a virgin through the Holy Spirit in defense against the Jewish accusation of illegitimacy.

One thing is certain, though: the translation 'I am a virgin' is 'loaded'. Why? Because it assumes Mary's conception while still a virgin. For this reason Fitzmyer translates *andra ou ginōskō* as 'I have no relations with a man'. This leaves the words of Mary in Luke as ambiguous as they are in the Greek text.

Conception through the Holy Spirit

The angel Gabriel responds to Mary's question in Lk. 1.34 about not having a man by saying, 'The Holy Spirit will come upon you, and the power of the Most High will overshadow you' (Lk. 1.35). 'Most High' is a Jewish metonym for God, frequently used in the Hebrew scriptures. In the New Testament it occurs most often in the writings of Luke, where it is used three times in the stories of Jesus' birth (Lk. 1.32, 35,

76) and in Lk. 6.35; Acts 7.48; 16.17. Matthew, who is certainly one of the most Jewish authors of the New Testament, does not use the word at all, and Mark uses it only in 5.7 (see Lk. 8.28).

The word 'come upon' (*eperchomai*) is peculiar to Luke among the Gospel writers, and it occurs elsewhere in the New Testament only in Eph. 2.7 and Jas 5.1. But Luke's use of the word with the Spirit is unique. Besides Lk. 1.35, he uses it in Acts 1.8 of the Holy Spirit coming upon the disciples. The same idea occurs in a variant form in Lk. 2.25: 'And the Holy Spirit rested on him'. Here the 'him' is Simeon, about whom Luke writes further: 'It had been revealed to him by the Holy Spirit that he would not see death before he had seen the Lord's Messiah' (Lk. 2.27). Simeon was also 'guided by the Spirit' (Lk. 2.27). In these passages, as in *Pss. Sol.* 17.36-37, the Holy Spirit is instrumental in determining the destiny of the Messiah.

There is no comparable passage in the Old Testament to the idea of the Holy Spirit 'coming upon' the person who was to give birth to the Messiah. However, in *Pss. Sol.* 17.37 the author does write about the Holy Spirit and the Messiah: 'For God will make him powerful by means of the Holy Spirit'. Compare Lk. 4.14: 'Then Jesus, filled with the power of the Spirit' (see also Isa. 11.2).

The phrase 'filled with the Holy Spirit' is also peculiar to Luke (but see Eph. 5.18). It occurs first in Lk. 1.15 in the words of the angel of the Lord to Zechariah about his son. Elsewhere in the birth narratives the phrase occurs in Lk. 1.41, 67. In the first passage 'Elizabeth was filled with the Holy Spirit'; and in the second, the same words are written about Zechariah (see also Acts 2.4; 4.8, 31; 7.55; 9.17; 13.9, 52).

Luke's word 'overshadow' (*episkiazō*) is rare in the Bible. Luke uses it in parallel with 'come upon' (Lk. 1.35), and it emphasizes the power of God's presence, as in Exod. 40.35 and the story of Jesus' transfiguration (Lk. 9.34; Mk 9.7; Mt. 17.5; see also Acts 5.15). Luke may also have intended the element of protection, as in Pss. 90.4 and 139.7, since the angel told Mary not to be afraid.

Since in Lk. 1.35 Holy Spirit and Most High are in parallel, some scholars have maintained that Luke thought of God himself as sharing physical union with Mary. If that was true, Luke was reflecting a mythical notion derived from Hellenistic authors. Two interesting passages from Plutarch, biographer and eclectic philosopher at the time of Luke, contain ideas similar to those of Luke in 1.35.

> Yet the Egyptians make a distinction which they think is not incredible, namely, that it is possible for a spirit of God to come near a woman and to create certain beginnings of generation, but there is not sexual intercourse (*Lives*, 'Numa' 4; see Mt. 1.18, 20, 25).

> And I do not think it terrible if God not coming near in the manner of a man, but by some other touches or through other contacts, alters the mortal nature and makes it pregnant with a more divine offspring (*Morals*, 'Symposiacs' 8.3).

With respect to the supernatural conception of Mary, there are two interesting passages in Philo that help to throw light on what Luke says. Concerning the pregnancy of Rebekah, the wife of Isaac, the Septuagint, following the Hebrew text, reads: 'And Isaac prayed to the Lord concerning Rebekah, his wife, because she was barren; and God heard him, and Rebekah his wife conceived in her womb' (Gen. 25.21). Rebekah, like Elizabeth (Lk. 1.8-25), became pregnant because the Lord heard the prayer of her husband. In each instance, of course, the woman obviously became pregnant in the usual manner—after sexual relations with her husband.

Now let us observe how Philo treats the story of Isaac and Rebekah: 'Isaac...besought God, and through the power of the one besought [that is, God] ... Rebekah became pregnant' (*Cher*. 13 [47]). Philo is not content to say only that the Lord heard Isaac's prayer. Philo implies a more direct influence from God, a special power. This becomes completely evident from the way Philo talks about the conception of Moses.

According to LXX Exod. 2.21-22, Moses' future father-in-law gave his daughter Zipporah to Moses for a wife. And then the text simply says: 'And the woman conceived and gave birth to a son'. About this incident, however, Philo says, 'Without supplication and prayer Moses, when he took Zipporah...found her pregnant through no mortal being' (*Cher*. 13 [47]).

The examples just given are close parallels to Luke's idea of the Spirit coming upon Mary. In each instance no human being is responsible for the pregnancy of the woman, but an external or supernatural power is. See here also the passages from Philo concerning Tamar quoted above in Chapter 2.

The quotations from Plutarch, a pagan, and Philo, a Hellenistic Jew, as well as the passages from the Septuagint, help us to understand where Luke was coming from when he wrote about Mary's conception as he did. This, coupled with the peculiar words and ideas of Luke, seems to indicate his creativity in composing the story of the conception of Jesus. And, in turn, we cannot ignore the bearing it has on the consideration of Luke's story of the annunciation of Jesus' birth as myth or history.

Chapter 4

THE USE OF OLD TESTAMENT MATERIAL

I have already made some observations about the use of the Old Testament by Matthew and Luke. Now I want to study the subject in more detail and raise some questions.

Matthew's Use of the Old Testament

According to Matthew, the events in the stories of Jesus' birth took place in order to fulfill Old Testament prophecy, beginning with the story of the conception of Jesus and ending with the story about his family going to live in Nazareth. Matthew's custom of narrating events as fulfillment of Old Testament prophecy differs from the method of Luke in his birth stories. Although Luke was very familiar with the Greek Old Testament, in his stories of Jesus' birth he never lets his readers know that he is directly quoting a passage from the Old Testament. In the body of his Gospel, though, Luke does use fulfillment quotations.

If the Old Testament passages quoted by Matthew were in an original core of material—if, indeed, there was such a core—why did Luke leave them out? And if they were not in such material, why did Matthew put them in? Although the poetic sections of Luke's stories are saturated with allusions to Old Testament sources, Luke has little in common with Matthew in the way he uses the Old Testament in his birth narratives.

As with the virgin birth of Jesus and the quotation from Isa. 7.14 in Mt. 1.23, the events reported in Matthew 2 also happened 'to fulfill' Old Testament prophecies. Fulfillment of prophecy is a special feature of Matthew's literary style and theological viewpoint not just in the birth narratives. Although Mark writes that Jesus was 'at home' in Capernaum (Mk 2.1), Matthew says, 'He [Jesus] left Nazareth and made his home in Capernaum...that what had been spoken through the prophet Isaiah might be fulfilled' (Mt. 4.13-14; see Isa. 8.23–9.1).

According to Matthew, Jesus 'cured all who were sick' in order 'to fulfill' another prophecy of Isaiah (Mt. 8.16-17; see also Isa. 53.4).[1]

Chiastic Pattern in Matthew 1 and 2

It has been suggested that Matthew organized the material in the stories of Jesus' birth, including the quotations from the Old Testament, according to a specific plan. I should like to suggest that there is a kind of chiastic pattern in the way the Old Testament quotations, dreams of Joseph, and narratives are alternated.[2]

1. Use of Old Testament—Jesus called the Messiah (1.2-16)	15. Use of Old Testament—Jesus called a Nazorean (2.23b)
2. Narrative (1.17-20a)	14. Narrative (2.21-23a)
3. Dream of Joseph (1.20b-21)	13. Dream of Joseph (2.19-20)
4. Quotation of Old Testament (1.22-23)	12. Quotation of Old Testament (2.17-18)
5. Narrative (1.24–2.5a)	11. Narrative (2.16)
6. Quotation of Old Testament (2.5b-6)	10. Quotation of Old Testament (2.15b)
7. Narrative (2.7-12)	9. Narrative (2.14-15a)

8. Dream of Joseph (2.13)

As with other plans, this one is not perfect. However, Matthew's motive of showing fulfillment of Old Testament prophecy and the chiastic arrangement of his material help to explain some of the differences between the accounts in the two Gospels. At the same time, Matthew's motive raises more problems with respect to the historical value of his narratives.

The Name 'Jesus'

One place where Matthew's use of the Old Testament is not so obvious as in his fulfillment quotations is in the naming of Jesus. Joseph is told by an angel of the Lord, 'You are to name him Jesus, for he will save his people from their sins' (Mt. 1.21).

We have learned that the name Jesus is the Greek form of the Hebrew *Joshua* (Aramaic, *Jeshua*), meaning 'Yahweh is salvation', 'Yahweh saves' or 'Yahweh will save'. According to Matthew, Jesus was 'king

1. For other fulfillment quotations from Isaiah see Mt. 12.17; 13.14, 35; 21.4; 26.54, 56; 27.9.

2. For plans others have suggested for Mt. 1.18–2.23, see Brown, *Birth*, pp. 48-54. If Brown has mentioned a chiastic plan, it has escaped my notice.

of the Jews', so he must be treated as a king and receive homage (Mt. 2.2, 8). Moreover, he must also act as a Hebrew king would be expected to act, especially in accordance with his name: 'for he will save his people from their sins'. Here Matthew was also influenced by Old Testament thought in such passages as, for example, 1 Sam. 10.25-27. There 'some worthless fellows' said about King Saul, 'How can this man save us?' (1 Sam. 11.1-11; see also 2 Sam. 5.1-10).

Matthew supports his view of Jesus as a savior-king with an allusion to LXX Ps. 130.8: 'And he [God] shall deliver Israel from all its sins'. In this way Matthew presents Jesus as the fulfillment of an Old Testament prediction without specifically saying so. Matthew's language is akin to that of Lk. 1.77: 'to give knowledge of salvation to his people by the forgiveness of their sins'. Does the close similarity mean Luke used Matthew, or, as with Matthew, was Luke also influenced by the Old Testament?

'Virgin' and 'Emmanuel'

The words 'the virgin' are the *hē parthenos* of the LXX Isa. 7.14 and not a translation of the word *hā'almâ*, 'the young woman', of the Hebrew text. Although both the Hebrew and Greek texts have the name Emmanuel, the explanation of it does not occur in either text. Because the name is a Hebrew word put into Greek letters, Matthew may have thought it necessary to explain its meaning.[3] However, it seems that his purpose was really christological. Matthew wanted his readers to think of Jesus as the representative of God among them. His statement of the last words of the resurrected Jesus to his disciples supports this supposition: 'And remember, I am with you always, to the end of the age' (Mt. 28.20). These words, only in Matthew's Gospel, give the disciples assurance that Jesus' presence will not have ceased with his disappearance from earth. The explanation of Emmanuel ties the beginning of Jesus' life in with the end of it and the birth story in with the rest of the Gospel. And the two passages, Mt. 1.23 and 28.20, form an inclusio.

An interesting difference between the text of the quotation from Isa. 7.14 in Matthew and any other text we have of it concerns the person who is to name the child. The Hebrew text says that the woman about

3. Matthew may, indeed, have found the meaning of Emmanuel in Isa. 8.8, 'with us is God', the order of words as in Matthew (see also Isa. 8.10), as suggested by Brown, *Birth*, pp. 152-53.

to bear the son shall name him: 'And she shall call his name Immanuel' (the Hebrew form of the name). Matthew could not use the feminine form of the Hebrew verb because he has Joseph, not Mary, name Jesus. The Greek text of the passage from Isaiah reads: 'And you [singular] shall call'. Matthew puts the verb in the plural form, 'They shall call', which also does not fit in with his statement that Joseph is the person who gives Jesus his name.

The observations just made, along with the one about the inclusio, indicate that the meaning of the name Emmanuel, 'God is with us', is an important issue Matthew wanted to convey to his readers. It was more important than the linguistic coordination with an Old Testament text. We have observed that Matthew used the quotation from Isaiah in the first place as a tactic in his defense against the Jewish accusation of the illegitimacy of Jesus. According to Matthew, Jesus is not an illegitimate child; he is the divine presence among humankind.

Context of Isaiah 7.14

Isaiah was predicting a special child who would have religious and political significance for the Hebrew people. That is why the child was to be named Emmanuel, 'God is with us'. In a time of great crisis, when the land of Judah was at war with Israel and Syria, about 735 BC, Isaiah spoke his prophecy. He found hope for divine deliverance in a sign from the Lord himself: 'The Lord himself will give you [Ahaz, King of Judah] a sign'. The sign is the young woman who is with child and will bear a son whose name is to be Immanuel. That child was to deliver the kingdom of Judah from its tumultuous times.

The child mentioned in Isaiah was to be born in the near future: 'He shall eat curds and honey by the time he knows how to refuse the evil and choose the good. For before the child knows how to refuse the evil and choose the good, the land before whose two kings you are in dread will be deserted' (Isa. 7.16). Here the ability to distinguish between good and evil is not to be taken in the moral sense of right or wrong. Rather, it means that by the time the child was weaned—at two or three years of age—he would be smart enough to let his parents know what kind of food he liked and what he didn't.

Isaiah was not prophesying the birth of Jesus of Nazareth about eight centuries later. But, at the same time, it is also obvious that Matthew believed Mary was 'the virgin' (*hē parthenos*) spoken of by the prophet Isaiah.

Although Luke does not have the quotation from Isa. 7.14, he does seem to be influenced by it, as the following passages show. I transliterate the Greek texts, so that you can compare the likenesses and differences among them.

Mt. 1.23: *idou hē parthenos en gastri hexei kai texetai huion, kai kalesousin to onoma autou Emmanouel.*
Look, the virgin shall conceive [lit. 'have in the womb'] and bear a son,
and they shall name him Emmanuel (NRSV trans.).

Isa. 7.14 (LXX B): *idou hē parthenos en gastri lēmpsetai kai texetai huion, kai kaleseis to onoma autou Emmanouel.*
Behold, the virgin shall conceive [lit. 'shall receive in the womb'] and will bear a son,
and you shall name him Emmanuel (my trans.).

Lk. 1.31: *idou syllēmpsē en gastri kai texē huion kai kaleseis to onoma autou 'Iēsoun.*
And now, you will conceive in your womb and bear a son,
and you will name him Jesus (NRSV trans.).

Obviously, there are similarities and differences among the three texts. Luke's *syllēmpsē* ('you will conceive') is closer to LXX B of Isa. 7.14 than Matthew's *hexei* (lit. 'she will have'). However, Matthew's *hexei* is the LXX A of Isa. 7.14, which is Goulder's reading. Goulder suggests that Luke substitutes *syllēmpsē* for *hexei* 'because the marvel he wishes to relate is a virgin girl conceiving, and not a virgin girl carrying a child'.[4] However, Luke's *syllēmpsē* could be from LXX B without making a substitution, which Goulder suggests, because there is no difference in meaning between Luke's verb *syllambanō* and the Septuagint's *lambanō*.

Moreover, Luke uses *syllambanō* also in Lk. 1.24 of Elizabeth's conceiving, although without *en gastri* ('in the womb'; so also in 1.36). However, in 2.21 Luke writes that at Jesus' circumcision he was named Jesus, 'the name given by the angel before he was conceived [*syllambanō*] in the womb'. Here the word translated 'womb' is *koilia*, which he uses also for 'womb' in Lk. 1.41, 42, 44; 11.27; and 23.29. We shall learn later that Luke likes to vary his language, even in the birth narratives. So what I have said in the paragraph before this may simply be due to Luke's fondness for linguistic variation.

4. Goulder, *Luke*, I, pp. 222-23.

The verb for 'bear' (*tiktō*) is the same in all texts, except for the change in person made necessary by the contexts. The word for 'call' (*kaleō*) is also the same in all texts. The LXX changes the Hebrew from 'she will call' to 'you will call', a reading acceptable to Luke, because it fits with the angel telling Mary what to do. Matthew has 'they will call', a reading hard to explain, since the angel had said to Joseph, 'you shall call', the reading of the LXX Isa. 7.14. Brown suggests that the 'they' is the 'people' mentioned in Mt. 1.21: 'He will save his people from their sins'.[5]

In order to learn how we might deal further, in a critical manner, with a problem like the 'they' in Matthew's quotation, please look now at Lk. 1.59-63. There, when John was about to be circumcised and named, neighbors and relatives of his family were present. And Luke says, 'They were going to name him Zechariah, after his father'. Their suggestion was refused, first by John's mother and then by Zechariah who wrote: 'His name is John'. This makes it unlikely that the 'they' in Mt. 1.23 is the 'people' mentioned in Mt. 1.21, does it not? Moreover, Luke says that at the time of Jesus' circumcision, 'He was called Jesus, the name given by the angel' (Lk. 2.21), not Emmanuel. And Matthew says that Joseph named the baby Jesus, not Emmanuel. In both Matthew and Luke the implication is that one or both parents had the responsibility for naming the boy. Moreover, as we have learned, for Matthew Emmanuel was symbolic, not real.

In light of what we have now learned, perhaps the 'they' in Mt. 1.23 is to be understood as those responsible for performing the task of the circumcision of Jesus. However, Matthew says nothing about the circumcision of Jesus, and Jesus was not named Emmanuel but Jesus. So then, after all this, perhaps it is better just to admit that sometimes we do not know the reason for things than to try to explain the inexplicable.

Place of Jesus' Birth

In Jewish tradition before the time of Jesus there is no evidence for a specific place of the Messiah's birth. According to *Pss. Sol.* 17.47, God already knew the Messiah, even though he was still to come: 'This will be the majesty of the king of Israel whom God knew; he will raise him up over the house of Israel'. The Messiah already existed and was known to God, but his arrival was still expected. This idea occurs also

5. Brown, *Birth*, p. 152; see also pp. 143-52.

in 2 Esd. 12.32: 'This is the Messiah whom the Most High has kept [secret] until the end of days, who will arise from the offspring of David, and will come and speak with them'.

This Jewish view of the secrecy of the Messiah and the place of his birth is stated also by some Jews 'of the people of Jerusalem' in the Gospel of John. They refuse to believe in Jesus because they know where he is from. They are reported as saying, 'Yet we know where this man is from; but when the Messiah comes, no one will know where he is from' (Jn 7.25-27).

The uncertainty of the place of the Messiah's birth is reflected in the wise men's question, 'Where is the child who has been born king of the Jews?' (Mt. 2.2), and in the inquiry of Herod, 'He inquired of them where the Messiah was to be born' (Mt. 2.4). Matthew's Christian response is put on the lips of 'the chief priests and scribes': 'They told him, "In Bethlehem of Judea; for so it has been written by the prophet" ' (Mt. 2.5).

Bethlehem. The fact that both Matthew and Luke mention that Jesus was born in Bethlehem may mean that city had already been established in earlier Christian tradition as the place of his birth. But each writer explains the occurrence differently. Here I consider Matthew's explanation; I shall consider Luke's explanation later (see also Lk. 2.1-7).

Although Matthew and Luke both report that Jesus was born in Bethlehem of Judea, interesting differences between the stories raise problems for the critical reader. Typically, Matthew reports that Jesus was born in Bethlehem to fulfill an Old Testament prophecy (Mt. 2.6):

> In Bethlehem of Judea; for so it has been written by the prophet: 'And you, Bethlehem, in the land of Judah, are by no means least among the rulers of Judah; for from you shall come a ruler who is to shepherd my people Israel'.

Most of this quotation is from Mic. 5.2 (see below), for which the Hebrew text (Mic. 5.1) for the first line of the quotation reads: 'But you, O Bethlehem of Ephrathah, who are one of the little clans of Judah'. The LXX Mic. 5.2 reads: 'And you, Bethlehem, house of Ephrathah, are least to be counted among the thousands of Judah'. No matter which text Matthew used, he changed the words to make them mean the opposite of the Old Testament text. Instead of 'one of the little clans' or 'least to be counted', Matthew writes 'by no means least'. He did this, of course, to make Bethlehem more prestigious as the place of Jesus' birth.

As the record stands, then, both Matthew and Luke report that Jesus was born in Bethlehem. Both writers believed that as the Messiah Jesus was a descendant of David. It was natural, I suppose, that since Bethlehem had been the hometown of David's family, for the authors to report the birth of the Messiah in that town. But each writer has a different reason for saying that the birth occurred there.

Bethlehem and the Nazareth Tradition. Along with the tradition of Jesus' birth in Bethlehem, a parallel tradition of Jesus' origin in Nazareth had already been established. Again, Matthew explains the Nazareth tradition as the fulfillment of Old Testament prophecy (Mt. 2.19-23). But because Luke took Joseph and Mary from Nazareth to Bethlehem for the registration (Lk. 2.1-7), it was only natural for him to have Joseph and his family return to Nazareth, 'their own town' (Lk. 2.39).

Matthew says nothing about Joseph and Mary traveling from Nazareth to Bethlehem. And about the wise men he says, 'On entering the house, they saw the child with Mary his mother' (Mt. 2.11). This statement gives the impression that Jesus' parents always lived in Bethlehem. According to Luke, on the other hand, Joseph and Mary lived in 'a town in Galilee called Nazareth' (Lk. 1.26). From Nazareth they traveled to Bethlehem, because of the registration decreed by Emperor Augustus. According to Luke, this journey was necessary because Joseph 'was descended from the house and family of David' (Lk. 2.4). According to Luke, then, because of Joseph's lineage, he and Mary went to Bethlehem, not because Jesus as the Messiah was to be born there.

It appears that Matthew knew nothing about the prior residence of Joseph and Mary in Nazareth of Galilee. Indeed, if we had only Matthew's account, we would have to assume that Bethlehem had been the home of Mary and Joseph before Jesus was born. Why? Because on entering the house, the wise men saw the child Jesus with his mother Mary (Mt. 2.11).

One must be careful not to read too much symbolism into Matthew's statement about the house and Mary. According to R.H. Gundry, ' "The house" means Jesus' house... The seeing of the child with Mary his mother reflects the tradition behind Luke 2:16-17' about Mary, Joseph and the child in the manger. 'But,' says Gundry, 'Joseph has dropped out'. But how can we say that 'the child has come forward in order of mention, and Mary has gained the designation "his mother," as in 1:18—all to emphasize Jesus' virgin birth and deity'?[6]

Matthew's statement about the house, child and Mary, with Joseph absent, may well be another indication of the illegitimacy of Jesus as seen through the eyes of Matthew's Jewish adversaries. Or if we take 'Jesus' house' as his home, as Gundry does in Mt. 4.13; 9.10; and 13.1,[7] then we can assume that Jesus was born in the house of (Joseph and) Mary in Bethlehem and that she (and Joseph) had always lived there.

Matthew gives no hint of the residence of Joseph and Mary in Nazareth before the birth of Jesus. According to Matthew that tradition, characteristically, developed as a fulfillment of Old Testament prophecy. Herod's son Archelaus, a scoundrel like his father, had come to power in Judea. After being warned in a dream, Joseph went to Galilee, where 'he made his home in a town called Nazareth' (Mt. 2.22-23). But the motive of scripture fulfillment colors what could conceivably be a historical account. Matthew's motive of scripture fulfillment becomes quite clear when he adds, 'so that what had been spoken through the prophets might be fulfilled, "He will be called a Nazorean"' (Mt. 2.23). The source of the quotation is uncertain, but see Judg. 13.5; 16.17; 1 Sam. 1.11, 22; Isa. 11.1.

Since Bethlehem occurs in both Matthew and Luke, that place for Jesus' birth may already have been fixed in Christian tradition before the stories of his birth were written. That is the view of Brown,[8] who denies that Luke knew Matthew and may have taken the idea of Bethlehem from him. Goulder gently chides Brown on that point.[9] We learn from Mark that Jesus' origin in Nazareth had been fixed in tradition: 'In those days Jesus came from Nazareth of Galilee and was baptized by John' (Mk 1.9). In the book of Acts, even in the earliest material, Jesus is referred to as 'Jesus of Nazareth' and 'Jesus Christ of Nazareth' (Acts 2.22; 3.6; 6.14; 10.38; 26.9).

The traditions of Bethlehem and Galilee are both reflected in a context of Christian controversy with the Jews in John 7. There the writer

6. R.H. Gundry, *Matthew: A Commentary on his Literary and Theological Art* (Grand Rapids: Eerdmans, 1982), p. 31.

7. Gundry, *Matthew*, pp. 167, 251.

8. Brown, *Birth*, pp. 411-14.

9. Goulder, *Luke*, I, p. 248.

reports that some people asked, 'Surely the Messiah does not come from Galilee, does he? Has not the scripture said that the Messiah is descended from David and comes from Bethlehem, the village where David lived?' (Jn 7.41-42; see also Jn 1.46). These statements clearly represent a Christian viewpoint. The Jewish view with respect to the origin of the Messiah is given earlier in Jn 7.26-27: 'Can it be that the authorities really know that this is the Messiah? Yet we know where this man is from; but when the Messiah comes, no one will know where he is from.' The point of controversy is that Jesus cannot be the Messiah because the Jews know from where he comes.

The view, as stated in Jn 7.26-27, that when the Messiah comes no one will know from where he comes is that of writers of Jewish apocryphal literature and of rabbinic Judaism. In that literature it is nowhere stated when or from where the Messiah will come. His coming may be either near or a long time away as indicated by certain signs. Men who are righteous might pray for the Messiah to come soon, but ultimately only God knows the exact time and place of his coming.

The use of any Old Testament text to support a specific place for the birth of Jesus as the Messiah is specifically Christian. Although Matthew places the reference to Jesus' birth at Bethlehem on the lips of chief priests and scribes (Mt. 2.3-5), and John on the lips of Jesus' Jewish critics, we must not assume that by the first century AD Jews had come to expect the birth of the Messiah in Bethlehem. The tradition of Jesus' birth at Bethlehem arose in Christian tradition; and after that happened, it continued to survive on the presumed authority of Old Testament scripture. No Jewish sources speak of Bethlehem as the place of the Messiah's birth before the fourth century AD.

Jesus' first followers were all Jews who believed that he was, indeed, their long-expected Messiah, the 'Son of David'. Once they believed that, it would be natural for them to believe that their Messiah was born in Bethlehem, especially in light of passages such as these: David was 'a son of Jesse the Bethlehemite' (1 Sam. 16.18), 'the son of an Ephrathite of Bethlehem in Judah' (1 Sam. 17.12), who fed 'his father's sheep at Bethlehem' (1 Sam. 17.15).

The Christian claim that their Messiah was born at Bethlehem ran counter to the Jewish belief that the place from where the Messiah was to appear was unknown. That claim gave rise to one of the arguments of the Jews that because the place of his birth was known Jesus was not the Messiah. So the Christians had to come up with counter-arguments.

Matthew found his defense by interpreting an Old Testament text in a unique way, and Jn 7.41-42 reflects the view of Matthew, which by John's time had become a part of Christian apologetic.

Micah 5.(1)2 is to be included among Old Testament passages that speak of an exceptional king to come who would be from the 'root of Jesse' (Isa. 11.10) and 'a shoot...from the stump of Jesse', the father of David (Isa. 11.1). Jeremiah writes of God raising 'up for David a righteous Branch' who 'shall reign as king and deal wisely' (Jer. 23.5; see also Zech. 3.8; 6.12). But the idea of a messianic king descended from the family of David is not the same thing as the belief that the Messiah would be born in Bethlehem. The passage in Micah means no more than that the expected messianic king would come from the family of David whose home had been in Bethlehem. It does not mean that Bethlehem was known to be the place of the Messiah's birth.

As a proof text from the Old Testament in his defense of Jesus' birth at Bethlehem Matthew conflates Mic. 5.(1)2 with 2 Sam. 5.2. Micah 5.1 (Hebrew) reads: 'From you he shall come forth to me that is to be a ruler in Israel'. The LXX Mic. 5.2 reads: 'From you he shall come forth to me to be a ruler of Israel'. The Hebrew of 2 Sam. 5.2 is: 'You shall indeed feed [shepherd] my people Israel, and you shall be for a ruler over Israel'. The LXX 2 Sam. 5.2 reads: 'You shall shepherd [feed, rule] my people Israel, and you shall be for a leader to my people Israel'. Here is Mt. 2.6b: 'for from you shall come a ruler who is to shepherd [rule] my people Israel'.

There is no essential difference between the Hebrew and Greek texts of 2 Sam. 5.2. Although Matthew has inverted the lines in the text of 2 Sam. 5.2, that is not a crucial point and probably means that he was quoting his text from memory and got a bit mixed up. The words 'for from you' in Matthew's text do not appear in either the Hebrew or Greek version of 2 Sam. 5.2. This is important for understanding the point Matthew wanted to make. He retained the words 'from you' from the text of Mic. 5.2 in order to make sure that his readers understood that from Bethlehem (Mt. 2.6) the Davidic Messiah Jesus has come.

The conflated quotation from Mic. 5.2 and 2 Sam. 5.2 is probably more fittingly adapted by Matthew to the context than any other quotation in his story of Jesus' birth. Although Matthew's readers may not have realized it, a couple of lines after those Matthew quotes from Micah there are words referring to a coming birth: 'When she who is in labor has brought forth' (Mic. 5.3).

Matthew 2.6, then, is a clear case of an independent Christian interpretation of Old Testament texts to argue a point. Herod's question, 'Where is the child who has been born king of the Jews?' (Mt. 2.2), represents the characteristic Jewish expectation of an ideal messianic king who was to rule over Israel. Yet the time and place of his coming were not known. With the second question, 'where the Messiah was to be born' (Mt. 2.4), and the answer of the priests and scribes, 'in Bethlehem of Judea', Matthew makes the transition from the characteristically Jewish to the uniquely Christian interpretation of the passages from Micah and 2 Samuel.

Contrary to the view of the Jews that Jesus cannot be the Messiah because they know where he comes from, Matthew says, 'O, yes he is!' Why? Because the scriptures prove that he was to be born at Bethlehem. His birth there happened just as the prophet Micah had predicted. And, besides that, according to Matthew, Jesus is to be a messianic ruler just as the words from 2 Sam. 5.2 prove.

Moreover, Jesus' residence in Nazareth of Galilee also fulfilled what other prophets had predicted: 'He will be called a Nazorean' (Mt. 2.23). But aware that it was difficult to find such a clear prophecy, Matthew uses the plural 'spoken through the prophets' (Mt. 2.23) instead of 'written by the prophet' (Mt. 2.5). In this way he had a better chance of not being wrong in his use of an Old Testament text.

It is impossible to tell what Old Testament passage or passages Matthew had in mind for the move to Nazareth, if, indeed, he actually had a specific passage or passages in mind at all. The problem of finding a specific text or texts is made the more difficult because Nazareth is not mentioned in any Jewish writing, including those of the Old Testament, before the New Testament was written. This is true in spite of the fact that there is archaeological evidence for habitation of the town for several centuries BC. Perhaps Matthew had in mind the Hebrew and/or Greek text of Judg. 16.17, but we just do not know for sure.

In the Hebrew text of Judg. 16.17 (in the Hebrew scriptures Judges is one of the Former Prophets) Samson says of himself: 'I have been a nazirite of God from my mother's womb' (see also Judg. 13.5, 7). The LXX B of Judg. 16.17 reads: 'I am a holy one [Greek, *hagios*] of God from my mother's womb', and LXX A reads: 'I am a nazirite [Greek, *nazeiraios*]'. Matthew 2.23 reads: 'He will be called a Nazorean [Greek, *nazōraios*]'. Matthew would not have needed a very vivid imagination to derive 'Nazareth' from either the Hebrew or Greek text of

Judg. 16.17 as the name of a place, especially since it did not occur in the Old Testament.

Matthew may have quoted an Old Testament text hitherto unknown to us. The news magazine *U.S. News & World Report* contains an article on the Qumran Scrolls.[10] In it an unnamed professor is quoted as saying, with respect to the Nazorean quotation in Mt. 2.23, 'The Qumran version 1 Samuel contains language that "is startlingly close."' The passage from 1 Samuel is not given, but it might be 1 Sam. 1.11 or 1.22.

Goulder says that in Mt. 2.23 Matthew 'seems to refer' to Samson's annunciation in Judg. 13.5: 'He shall be a Nazirite'. Since Jesus came eating and drinking and John the Baptist did not (Lk. 7.34; see also Mt. 11.18-19), the text in Matthew 'is certainly much more suited to John', about whom Luke writes: 'He must never drink wine or strong drink' (Lk. 1.15).[11]

Determining the source of the quotation, however, becomes even more complicated. A curious thing is that in his birth stories Luke actually mentions holiness (see LXX Judg. 16.17 above) with reference to Jesus. The angel tells Mary, 'The child to be born will be holy' (Lk. 1.35). This ties the birth stories in with the body of the Gospel in Lk. 4.34, where the demon in a man recognizes Jesus as 'the Holy One of God' (see also Mk 1.24).

If Matthew was aware that Jesus had become known as 'the Holy One of God', he may have had in mind certain Greek texts of Judg. 16.17 where 'holy' (*hagios*: LXX A) and 'Nazirite' (*nazeiraios*: LXX B) are mentioned. Or, Matthew may have had in mind the Hebrew or Greek text of Isa. 4.3 that the remnant left in Jerusalem 'will be called holy' when the day of 'the branch of the Lord' comes. I would think, though, that if Matthew did have in mind the holiness of Jesus, along with the Nazorean idea, he would have mentioned it. Moreover, in contrast to Luke, Matthew never refers to the holiness of Jesus, either in his birth stories or in the body of the Gospel. Does this make it unlikely, then, that Matthew had the concept of the holiness of Jesus in mind when he used the Nazorean quotation?[12]

10. 7 July 1997, pp. 70-71.

11. Goulder, *Luke*, I, p. 209.

12. For more detailed discussion of the changes Matthew makes in the texts of Mic. 5.2 and 2 Sam. 5.2, as well as other Old Testament quotations in Mt. 2 and the problems involved, see Brown, *Birth*, pp. 184-88, 207-25.

The Manger and the Inn

Luke's story of the inn and the manger has a bearing on the specific place of Jesus' birth in Bethlehem, so I discuss it now.

There is nothing in the text of Lk. 2.6-7 about a stable or sheep or donkeys or cattle or other stage props Christians see in Christmas scenes. Moreover, in the city of Bethlehem there would not have been barns, as we are apt to think of them, with a variety of animals kept under the same roof in relatively comfortable quarters.

The word translated as 'manger' (Greek, *phatnē*) means 'stall' or 'feeding trough'. The fact that the text does say 'Mary laid him in a manger' suggests that the meaning 'feeding trough' is intended. And from what one sees while traveling in Israel, the feeding trough was usually under the open sky or, at best, under a crude lean-to.

Of New Testament writers only Luke uses the word *phatnē*, 'manger' (Lk. 2.7, 12, 16; 13.15). He surely intends it to stand in contrast to the word 'inn', in which there was no room for Joseph and Mary. However, we must not think of the word translated as 'inn' (*katalyma*) as some fancy place like the hotels or motels or bed and breakfast houses we might call inns. *Katalyma* would be better translated as 'lodging place'.[13]

In the time of Joseph and Mary people in Palestine traveled on foot or rode donkeys. There were many lodging places of the kind Luke mentions, rather crude resting places with roofs for shelter from the weather, especially the hot sunshine, where travelers could rest and probably sleep.

Only Luke tells the widely known parable of 'The Good Samaritan' who took the Jewish traveler to an inn, and took care of him (Lk. 10.34). There Luke uses the word *pandocheion* for 'inn', a higher-class place of lodging with an innkeeper or inn manager (see also Lk. 10.35). Travelers could stay in such inns overnight and also get something to eat.

We know about *pandocheion* as an inn, for example, from two stories of traveling Greek teachers who were contemporaries of Jesus. The teacher and miracle worker Apollonius of Tyana and some companions were traveling and were about to enter Rome. Philostratus, the biographer of Apollonius, writes: 'They found lodging in an inn [*pandocheion*] and were having their supper...' (*Life of Apollonius* 4.39). Epictetus, Greek Stoic philosopher and teacher, said to his students, 'So long as God gives something to you, take care of it as if it belonged to

13. Or as Brown has it, 'in the lodgings' (*Birth*, pp. 393, 399-401).

another, as those do who stay in an inn' (*pandocheion*; *Manual* 11). The inn mentioned in these stories is not the kind of inn (*katalyma*) Luke writes about in the story of Jesus' birth. There the point Luke probably wanted his readers to understand is that Jesus was born under very modest circumstances.

The word *katalyma* occurs in Mk 14.14 and Lk. 22.11, where it is sometimes taken as 'guest room' (NRSV; REB, 'room'). On the basis of those passages and other evidence, P. Benoit suggested years ago in a lecture at St Mary's Seminary in Baltimore, Maryland, where I was present, that *katalyma* should be understood as 'guest room' in Lk. 2.7: 'There was no place for them in the guest room'.[14] In the Septuagint the word is probably best understood as 'inn' or 'lodging' in Exod. 4.24; 1 Sam. 1.18; 9.22; Jer. 14.8; 40(33).12; Ezek. 23.21; Sir. 14.25; 1 Macc. 3.45.

Goulder suggests that Judg. 19.15 may have influenced Luke in Lk. 2.7. According to Judges, a Levite and his concubine turned aside from the road and sat down in the town of Gibeah, 'but no one took them in to spend the night' (LXX A, *katalysai*, a verb; see Luke's *katalyma*). However, LXX B reads *aulisthēnai* ('bivouac', 'spend the night'). Luke uses *kataluō* in the sense of 'find lodging' or 'lodge' in Lk. 11.12 and 19.7 and *auliizomai* in Lk. 21.37, so he was familiar with both words. Did Luke choose the reading of one manuscript over another? I suppose he could have. That may be one reason why Goulder feels it is hopeless 'to scour the Greek Bible for texts that might have inspired so famous a tale'. Yet he seems to do it many times.

Nevertheless, Goulder's final suggestion is appealing. He finds it in Mt. 8.20: 'Foxes have holes, and birds...have nests, but the Son of Man has nowhere to lay his head' (see also Lk. 9.58). As with John, 'who came neither eating nor drinking' (Mt. 11.18), 'how natural that he [Jesus] should have been laid where the animals eat, and found no place for his head among men'.[15]

It is obvious that Luke used many Old Testament texts in the composition of his birth stories. In my scouring for a text behind Lk. 2.7 I found Ezek. 21.30 intriguing. There the Lord says to Ezekiel: 'Turn

14. Benoit subsequently discussed his thesis in an article, '"*Non erat eis locus in diversorio" (Lc 2,7)*', in A. Descamps and A. de Halleux (eds.), *Mélanges Beda Rigaux* (Gembloux: Duculot, 1970), pp. 173-86.

15. Goulder, *Luke*, I, pp. 250-51. Brown, of course, and Fitzmyer do not agree that Luke knew Matthew. Their view is still the prevailing one.

aside, do not rest [*katalysēs*] in this place in which you were begotten; in your own land I will judge you'. There are linguistic parallels between that passage and Luke's narrative:

Ezekiel	*Luke*
apostrephe, 'turn aside'	*epestrepsan*, 'they turned back' or 'returned' (Lk. 2.39)
me katalysēs, 'do not lodge'	*ouk en topos en tō katalymati*,
en tō topō toutō, 'in this place'	'there was no place in the lodging' (Lk. 2.7)
en tē gē te idia sou, 'in your own land'	*eis polin heautōn*, 'in their city' (Lk. 2.39)
ho gegennēsai, 'where you were born'	*egennēsen huion*, 'she gave birth to a son' (Lk. 1.57; see also 1.13, 35)

Luke writes that Joseph and Mary 'returned to Galilee, to their own town of Nazareth' (Lk. 2.39). Instead of the move to Nazareth to fulfill Old Testament prophecy as with Matthew, did Luke want his readers to find symbolism in the inn episode and the return (*epestrepsan*) to Nazareth? Was Joseph to turn away from the land where he was born, the land of the Jews, and take Jesus back to Nazareth in Galilee, the land of the Gentiles (see Mt. 2.22; 4.15; see Isa. 9.1)? This, of course, is only a suggestion, but it is made plausible by Simeon's praise when Jesus was only eight days old: 'a light for revelation to the Gentiles, and for glory to your people Israel' (Lk. 2.32; see discussion of this verse later). Sometimes we can only suggest what Matthew or Luke or some other New Testament writer means. But stating a suggestion is different from making an assertion, for which there is often no good evidence either.

In Lk. 2.7 we read that after Mary gave birth to Jesus she 'wrapped him in bands of cloth, and laid him in a manger'. The word translated as 'bands of cloth' is really a verb (*sparganoō*), which means to 'swathe' or to 'swaddle'. 'Swaddle' means to 'wrap (a baby) with swaddling clothes', narrow strips of cloth used to wrap a baby to limit movement. The word is used in the New Testament only in Lk. 2.7, 12. Consider for a moment the circumstances surrounding Jesus' birth, including traveling such a long way by donkey so close to the time of Mary's delivery, the baby in a manger, and so on. Where would Mary have gotten such strips of cloth? Would she have brought them with her? Would some fellow traveler have given them to her?

In the Jewish apocryphal/deuterocanonical writing known as the Wisdom of Solomon, the writer, identifying himself with King Solomon, says, 'In swaddling clothes I was nourished with care' (Wis. 7.4). Did Luke even think about such cloths? Or did he just want to show descriptively that by swaddling her son Mary was being a caring mother?

Some Questions Remaining. Matthew has uniquely interpreted Old Testament Scripture to make a defense against a Jewish accusation, this time not about Jesus' conception and lineage but about his origins in Bethlehem and Nazareth. According to Matthew's adversaries, Jesus cannot be the Messiah because the place of his birth is known. Against a double-barreled volley Matthew has fired a double-barreled reply. And he has cleverly manipulated his weapon, Old Testament texts, to strengthen his attack.

So, if we think historically, as well as religiously, we have to raise several questions. Was Jesus really born in Bethlehem? If he was born in Bethlehem, did early Christians interpret Mic. 5.2 as they wished to support belief in Jesus' messiahship in light of his birth there? Or, did early Christians see in Mic. 5.2 a prediction of the Messiah's birth at Bethlehem and then invent the story of Jesus' birth there to fulfill the Old Testament prophecy? And what about the Nazareth tradition? Does Matthew's Old Testament quotation, even though we do not know the source of it, give some support to the view of Jesus' going there to live, as Matthew says, or not? On the other hand, does the lack of Old Testament support make the Lukan tradition of the residence of Jesus' parents in Nazareth before his birth in Bethlehem historical or not? Are the statements in Luke that there was no room in the inn and that Jesus was laid in a manger to be accepted as historical or not because there is no Old Testament prophecy about those things? Did Luke write the story of no place in the inn, with the return to Galilee, as symbolism for Jesus' work among Gentiles as well as among Jews?

We have learned that Josephus refers to the house of Rahab the prostitute as an inn (*katagōgion*), which has the same general meaning as Luke's *katalyma*, resting place or lodging place. So, I have some more questions. Did Luke say there was no place for Joseph and Mary in the inn, then, because inns were sometimes frequented by prostitutes and, therefore, he did not want Mary to be associated with such a place? This would be especially true if he was aware of the Jewish accusation of the illegitimacy of Jesus. And could it be for the same reason that he always has Joseph appearing with Mary as the father of Jesus?

Luke's Use of the Old Testament

One of the axioms among those who study the New Testament is that the better one knows the Old Testament the better one can understand the New Testament. This is particularly true for the study of Luke's stories of the annunciation and birth of Jesus. The reason for this is that Luke's use of the Old Testament in these stories is more concealed and subtle than that of Matthew. If we study Luke's stories carefully, we observe that several narratives from the Old Testament seem to be his models.

It has been demonstrated that the Old Testament narratives of the annunciation and birth of Isaac, Samuel and Samson have served as the basis for Luke's stories of the annunciation and birth of both John and Jesus. The narrative of Elkanah and his wife Hannah and their son Samuel was one model for Luke's stories of John and Jesus. The table below shows the parallels. Because the parallels are numerous, I may have missed some of them. As elsewhere, I use the NRSV, although sometimes the parallels are even closer in the original texts, some of which I translate a bit more literally.

Parallels between Birth Stories of Samuel and Jesus

1 Samuel 1–2	*Luke 1–2*
There was a certain man whose name was Elkanah (1.1)	There was a certain [Greek] priest named Zechariah (1.5)
The name of the one [wife] was Hannah (1.2)	Her name was Elizabeth (1.5)
Elkanah and Hannah had no children, the Lord had closed her womb (1.2, 6)	Zechariah and Elizabeth had no children ...because Elizabeth was barren (1.7)
Elkanah used to go up year by year from his town to worship and to sacrifice to the Lord (1.3)	Every year Jesus' parents went to Jerusalem for the festival of the Passover (2.41)
Elkanah and his family went up to offer to the Lord the yearly sacrifice (1.21)	And they offered a sacrifice (2.4)
Samuel's parents went up to the sanctuary at Shiloh to sacrifice, then they went back to their house at Ramah (1.3, 19)	Jesus' parents went up to the temple in Jerusalem every year, and then they went down to Nazareth, their own town (2.39, 41-42, 51)

1 Samuel 1–2	*Luke 1–2*
Hannah receives answer to her prayer from the priest Eli in the sanctuary at Shiloh (1.17)	Zechariah receives answer to his prayer from the angel in the sanctuary of the temple in Jerusalem (1.13)
Hannah, whose name means 'favor', says to Eli, 'Let your servant find favor in your sight' (1.18)	Gabriel addresses Mary as 'favored one' and says, 'You have found favor with God' (1.28, 30)
Hannah calls herself the servant of the Lord (1.11)	Mary calls herself the servant of the Lord (1.38)
'When the days were right' (Greek), Hannah conceived and bore a son (1.20)	'When the days were fulfilled for her to give birth, she bore her firstborn son' (Greek; 2.6-7)
	Elizabeth conceived...and she bore a son (1.24, 57)
She named him Samuel (1.20)	Elizabeth said: 'He is to be called John' 1.60)
	'He was called Jesus' (2.21)
And the boy Samuel grew up in the presence of the Lord (2.21)	The child grew and became strong ... and the favor of God was upon him (2.40)
The boy Samuel continued to grow both in stature and in favor with the Lord and with the people (2.26)	Jesus increased in wisdom and in stature, and in favor with God and humans (2.52)
Eli was very old (2.22)	Zechariah says, 'I am an old man' (1.18)
	Old age of Simeon is implied (2.26)
The woman [Hannah] went into her *katalyma* and ate and drank with her husband (1.18)	There was no place for them in the *katalyma* (2.7)
Hannah conceived because the Lord remembered her (1.19-20)	Elizabeth conceived because the Lord looked favorably on her (1.24-25)
Hannah says of unborn Samuel, 'He will drink no wine nor strong drink' (Greek; 1.11)	Angel says of the unborn John, 'He must never drink wine or strong drink' (1.15)
Eli blessed Elkanah and his wife because of their son (2.20)	Simeon blessed Joseph and Mary because of their son (2.34)

1 Samuel 1–2	*Luke 1–2*
After Hannah weaned Samuel, she brought him to the house of the Lord at Shiloh, along with the proper offerings. Hannah says, 'I have lent him to the Lord' (1.24-28)	After eight days and Jesus was circumcised, his parents brought him to Jerusalem, along with the proper offerings, to present him to the Lord (2.21-24)
Women served at the entrance to the tent of meeting (2.22; see also Exod. 38.8)	Anna never left the temple, but worshiped there night and day (2.37)
The boy Samuel was ministering to the Lord under Eli in the sanctuary (2.18; 3.1)	At twelve years of age Jesus was in his Father's house listening to the teachers and asking them questions (2.46-50)

The parallels listed show how close Luke's stories of the annunciation and birth of John and Jesus are to the story of the annunciation and birth of Samuel. The parallels also demonstrate that Luke's method of using the Old Testament in the birth narratives differs from that of Matthew. And we must always remember the element of Luke's creativity, which these parallels clearly substantiate.

In Jewish literature the temple in Jerusalem was often the scene for an appearance of God or an angel. Samuel's mother Hannah was in the sanctuary when she received the message from Eli the priest that God had heard her prayer for a son and that it would be granted. The Lord spoke to the boy Samuel in the temple (1 Sam. 3.1-14). Jesus was in the temple as a boy conversing with the teachers. Isaiah was in the temple when he received a call from the Lord to be a prophet after he had a spectacular vision (Isa. 5.1-13). And Zechariah received his message about the conception of his son from an angel while in the temple (Lk. 1.8-20).

Josephus tells a story very similar to Luke's narrative of Zechariah when writing about the high priest John Hyrcanus: 'Concerning the high priest Hyrcanus a story has been passed on about how the Deity spoke to him when he was alone as high priest in the temple burning incense' (*Ant.* 13.10.3). The story from Josephus shows that Luke's story of Zechariah in the temple is not unique. It also shows that such kinds of stories were not confined to the Bible.

Finally, we should observe that Luke forms an inclusion with his stories of Jesus' birth (Lk. 1.5–2.38). He begins by telling of an old, righteous, law-observing man and woman, Zechariah and his wife Elizabeth. The stories end with 'the righteous and devout' old man Simeon and the aged Anna who worshiped constantly in the temple. Part of the inclusion is the temple in Jerusalem as the locale for the beginning and end of the stories. The story of Samuel also begins and ends with the sanctuary of the Lord at Shiloh.

If we take these observations into account, along with the numerous parallels listed in the table above, it becomes obvious that the story of Samuel's birth and youth was the basic model for Luke's stories of John and Jesus.

Although it is universally agreed that Luke's language has been strongly influenced by the Septuagint, Goulder makes a point too often overlooked. He lists parallels between the vision of Zechariah and those of Cornelius and Peter (Acts 10.1–11.18) and says that Luke has a natural way about telling a tale, 'whether or not there is an Old Testament model' behind it. For Goulder, Mark was the primary source from which Luke got the 'germ of the idea' which gave the structure for Luke 1–2. And 'some things have been drawn in from Matthew as well'.[16] Anyhow, the creative way Luke uses the Old Testament in his birth narratives most distinguishes his method from that of Matthew.[17]

16. Goulder, *Luke*, I, pp. 205-207.

17. For more detailed study of the use of the Old Testament in Luke's stories of Jesus' birth see Brown, *Birth*, pp. 235-495; Fitzmyer, *Gospel*, I, pp. 303-448; and Goulder, *Luke*, I, pp. 205-91.

Chapter 5

Individual Pericopes in Matthew's Stories

Background Christology

'Pericope' (from the Greek *perikopē*, 'cutting all around'; then 'section', 'passage') is a term scholars use when referring to a unit or section of biblical text, usually complete in itself. Each pericope must be considered in light of the developing Christology of the early Christian church as it is reflected by each author in his own way. If we examine individual units carefully, we can sometimes think of possibilities about why and how the material came to be incorporated into the Gospels.

As we learn from Paul's letters and the book of Acts, within primitive Christianity Jesus came to be regarded as divine, that is, Son of God, Lord, and Savior, the bringer of salvation to humankind. These views came about as the result of the interpretation of Jesus' death as atonement for human sin, and especially the conviction that he rose from the dead (see, e.g., 1 Thess. 4.14; 1 Cor. 6.14; 15.3-8; 2 Cor. 4.13-14; Gal. 1.1; Rom. 1.4; 4.24-25; 10.8-13; Acts 2.24-36; 5.30-32; 13.32-39). As traditions about Jesus developed, his uniqueness was pushed backward to other points in his life, then all the way back to his birth. And, as we have already learned, the writer of the prologue to the fourth Gospel presents Jesus as pre-existing with God, even before the creation of the world.

We do not know whether Mark was aware of the traditions of Jesus' birth. What we do know, however, is that he wrote a Gospel in which the first verse is a dynamic statement of the writer's faith: 'The beginning of the good news [gospel] of Jesus Christ, the Son of God' (Mk 1.1). According to Mark, the first proof of Jesus' sonship comes at his baptism, not with his birth. Just as Jesus 'was coming up out of the water', a voice from heaven proclaimed, 'You are my Son, the Beloved; with you I am well pleased' (Mk 1.11). In contrast to Mark, Matthew and Luke, perhaps because of their own theological convictions, devoted two chapters to showing the uniqueness of Jesus before his baptism. They do this by telling of the unusual circumstances surrounding his conception and birth, as they received and perceived them from their sources. Then each author composed the stories in his own creative way.

Because of the manifest theological convictions of their authors, the Gospels are generally understood primarily as theological works. They are not, therefore, to be considered as histories or even as biographies, although they do contain some historical and biographical information. As I mentioned earlier, Horsley proposes 'a concept of realistic or history-like narrative' for understanding the birth narratives.[1] The stories of Jesus' birth and early life, which is only in Luke, do give the semblance of being biographical material, even though we cannot be certain of their historical veracity.

The Star

We have already dealt with the genealogies and the annunciation and birth of Jesus (Mt. 1.18-25; Lk. 1.26-38; 2.1-7). Now we consider several other individual pericopes in Matthew's stories.

The story that a special star arose in the east, moved westward to Jerusalem, then southward to Bethlehem, and stopped precisely over the place where the baby Jesus was is too much to believe. There is no proven record of any astrological phenomenon that comes close to the kind Matthew describes. So how can we best explain his use of the star?

There were popular beliefs that the birth of a great man was signaled by some special heavenly portent. Cicero reports a legend about the temple of Diana in Ephesus burning the night Alexander was born. According to Cicero, Alexander was born supernaturally by divine origin, as Egyptian legend had it. After his birth, when daylight broke, the magicians cried out that the plague and destruction of Asia had been born that night (Cicero, *De div.* 1.23.47).

Suetonius wrote that a portent appeared before the birth of Augustus indicating that a boy was to be born who would rule over Rome. The Roman senators became scared because of their own political ambitions and forbade the rearing of male children for a year, but the boy was saved from those who sought his life (*Lives of the Caesars*, 'Augustus' 2.94.3). Plutarch reported spectacular phenomena at the birth of

1. Horsley, *Liberation*, pp. 18-19.

Alexander the Great. The night he was born the temple of Artemis in the city of Ephesus burned while its priestess was away assisting at the birth of the baby. When day dawned, the magicians ran about the city and cried out that the day had brought forth something that would cause ruin and be fatal for all of Asia (Plutarch, *Lives*, 'Alexander' 3).

Matthew may have been aware of such popular beliefs. He surely knew the Old Testament metaphor of a star as a special deliverer who was to come. Among the various views that have been suggested to explain the appearance of the star at the time of Jesus' birth, the best is probably that Matthew was influenced by the story of Balaam and a passage from his oracles (Num. 22–24).[2]

As with the wise men, Balaam was a non-Jew, who, as with the wise men also, came 'from the east' (*ap' antolōn*, LXX Num. 23.7; so also Mt. 2.1). Compare Mt. 2.2: 'in the east' (*en tē anatolē*; see also Mt. 8.11). Balaam 'went back to his place' (Num. 24.25), and the wise men 'left for their own country' (Mt. 2.12).

Matthew was probably most influenced by a sentence in LXX Num. 24.17: 'A star shall rise out of Jacob, and a man shall stand up out of Israel; and he shall crush the leaders of Moab'. As if Herod knew this prediction—and perhaps he did—Matthew says, 'He was frightened, and all Jerusalem with him' (Mt. 2.3). Matthew might have said, though, that Herod was scared because he was aware of the popular beliefs about the births of great men and that such awareness was the reason he murdered persons that threatened his own rule.

The last clause in the quotation from Num. 24.17 makes it quite clear that the star or the man to come was to be born in the near future, not centuries later. As a kingdom that threatened the Israelites, Moab was long gone by the time of Matthew. By his time, though, the Jews used Num. 24.17 with reference to the coming of the Messiah, as we know from a particular passage in the Qumran Scrolls. The Jews in the community at Qumran who were expecting two Messiahs wrote that the star is 'the Interpreter of the Law'. Instead of 'a man', as in LXX Num. 24.17, the Hebrew text reads, 'a scepter'. According to the Damascus Document from Qumran, the scepter is 'the Prince of all the Congregation' (CD 7.18-20). 'The Interpreter of the Law' would be the Priestly Messiah, and 'the Prince', the royal or Davidic Messiah. In the *Testaments of the Twelve Patriarchs* the passage from Num. 24.17 is

2. For various views about the star see Brown, *Birth*, pp. 170-74, 190-96, 610-13.

also used with reference to the messianic rulers who are to come (*T. Levi* 18.1-14; *T. Jud.* 24.1-6).

Matthew was probably most influenced by the story of Balaam and the prediction of the star and the man or scepter to come. However, it is not improbable that he was also influenced by legends that were developing about famous Hebrew men. Here is a legend about Abraham.

The birth of Abraham had been seen in the stars by a king named Nimrod. He had a kingdom in Mesopotamia and became a notorious character in legends known throughout the ancient Near East. According to one of the legends, preserved in Gen. 10.8-12, Nimrod 'was the first on earth to become a mighty warrior. He was [also] a mighty hunter before the Lord.'

According to a later Jewish legend, it had been revealed to Nimrod through the stars that a man would be born to rise up against him and expose the falsity of his religion. Frightened by what he had seen in the stars, Nimrod consulted his advisers, who agreed to a man that he should build a big house. Then he was to invite all pregnant women and their midwives to the house. Nimrod did precisely as advised in every respect. When the time of each woman came to give birth, it was the responsibility of the midwife to kill every boy baby. All female babies were to be spared. Guards were stationed around the house to prevent any woman from escaping. All boy babies were killed at their mothers' breasts. But women who gave birth to girls were dressed in the finest clothes and escorted from the house with great honors. More than 70,000 children were killed in that manner.

Angels appeared to God and appealed to him to do something to stop the slaughter of the children. God promised to punish Nimrod. Meanwhile, the pregnant wife of Terah, the father-to-be of Abraham, left the city greatly afraid. She wandered toward the desert until she found a cave. There, the next day, she gave birth to a son. 'The mother rejoiced exceedingly. The babe she bore was our father Abraham'.[3]

Aspects of legends like this appear in Matthew's story of Jesus' birth. His stories of Herod, the wise men, and the murder of the children are not so detailed as the Abraham legend. We must remember, though, that Matthew's stories were motivated primarily by his concern for presenting Jesus as the fulfillment of Old Testament prophecy and by his own christological views.

3. Ginzberg, *Legends*, I, pp. 186-88.

Herod and the Wise Men

The biggest break in Matthew's birth stories comes at the end of ch. 1. This observation gives support to the view that Matthew used the genealogy of Jesus and composed the story of his virginal conception to counter the Jewish accusation of Jesus' illegitimacy. Next Matthew used the dreams of Joseph and the further portrayal of Jesus as the fulfillment of Old Testament prophecy in order to demonstrate the hand of God in saving the child Messiah from the wiles of Herod.

Matthew 2.1-23 is a larger section comprised of two pericopes Herod and the wise men (Mt. 2.1-12), and Herod and the flights to Egypt and Nazareth (Mt. 2.13-23). The increasing hostility of Herod to the family of Jesus, their flight to Egypt and their return to Israel at the death of Herod give a logical sequence to the two pericopes in Matthew 2. Herod, with his son Archelaus, is the unifying factor.

In the story of Herod and the wise men two statements in particular provide insight into Matthew's thought. As 'king of the Jews' (Mt. 2.2) Jesus has been rejected by his own people, Israel, symbolized by Herod. On the other hand, the wise men manifest a positive reaction to 'the child who has been born king of the Jews' (Mt. 2.2). The wise men knelt down, paid homage to Jesus and gave him gifts. In doing so, they represent those Gentiles who accepted Jesus as Matthew understood him.

Matthew directs the statements about Herod and the wise men to his skeptical, even critical, fellow Jews as further proof of Jesus' messiahship. At the same time, Matthew has in mind especially those Jews, and Gentiles as well, who might be thinking of becoming converts to the Jesus movement. The theme of Jewish rejection and Gentile acceptance of Jesus is a prominent one throughout Matthew's Gospel, beginning with the stories of Jesus' birth.

Brown[4] and I agree on the symbolism of Herod representing the Jews who rejected Jesus, but Horsley does not agree. He says, 'Herod is Herod, and the Magi are the Magi in Matthew 2'. Therefore, it is absurd to take 'them as representatives of something else'. It may be true, as Horsley says, that Herod and Pilate were aware of 'the challenge posed by Jesus "the king of the Jews"' to their own power.[5] Yet, there are problems with Horsley's view.

4. Brown, *Birth*, pp. 180-83.
5. Horsley, *Liberation*, pp. 7-8.

At the end of Part 2 of his book Horsley does acknowledge the religious or evangelistic element in the stories of Jesus' birth, which he calls stories of liberation. However, Horsley greatly neglects the religious aspect as he goes along. Granted, 'Herod is Herod', but what is Herodian about his desire to go and pay the newly born Messiah homage (Mt. 2.8), especially if Jesus was to challenge his own rule? Why would Matthew ever write a statement like that, since it was surely contrary to everything he would have known about Herod, if not for an evangelistic purpose?

Again, granted, the stories may partly 'focus on the redemption of Israel from its rulers'. But is it true to say that 'the irreducible basis of the story' in Matthew 2 'has to be the opposition of the threatened king Herod to the child Jesus'? Again, we must ask: Why, then, would Herod want to go to pay Jesus homage (Mt. 2.7-8)? Each separate story has to be taken in the context of the whole. Are the stories really devoid of religious or theological concerns, as may be implied from what Horsley usually says?

What about 'he will save his people from their sins' (Mt. 1.21)? It is partly true that 'Luke clearly understands Jesus to be in direct confrontation with the emperor' Augustus. But was the 'Savior, who is the Messiah, the Lord' (Lk. 2.11), only an irreducible indication of liberation from political rulers and class conflict? And was the message of Jesus as 'good news for the whole people' the 'gospel of *liberation*' for a people subjected to the Roman world order only liberation from 'Roman military might'?[6]

Luke seems to have thought the good news (Lk. 1.19; 2.10) was more than that. The tradition of 'good news' from the Lord (Isa. 40; 52–53; 60–61) was a liberation from military overlords, but it also included a subsequent era of peace, justice and righteousness for all. The peace Jesus came to bring (Lk. 2.14; see discussion of Luke's 'peace' below) was not just peace from hostile conflict, was it?

What Kinds of Persons Were Wise Men?

Matthew does not identify the wise men, so we cannot do so. However, we know something about such characters in general.

'Wise men' translates one Greek word (*magoi*), singular *magos*. One of the earliest meanings of the term was 'quack', as in Sophocles's drama, *Oedipus, King of Thebes*, where Oedipus calls the soothsayer 'a

6. Horsley, *Liberation*, pp. 14-15, 33, 40.

tricky quack'. *Magos* did not mean the same thing for the ancients as for us. Nor did the term *mageia*, from which the words 'magic' and 'magician' come. Both of those terms came into the Greek language from Persia. The *magoi* were respected priests similar to those in the Hebrew scriptures. *Mageia* literally means 'theology of the magicians'.[7]

There is an abundance of literature on the magi from the ancient Mesopotamian world, but less from Syria and pre-Israelite Canaan (Palestine). In polytheistic cultures humans turned to magic because the gods did not satisfy all their needs and desires.

The word *magos* occurs in the Septuagint only in the book of Daniel, whose setting is the land of the East, the land of Matthew's Magi. In Dan 2.2 King Nebuchadnezzar summoned the enchanters, the magi (*magous*; 'magicians'), and the sorcerers (*pharmakous*; see below). However, the Hebrews also practiced magic. We are most familiar, perhaps, with the characters of Egypt in the stories of Moses and the Pharaoh. Moses and Aaron performed tricks, and so did the Egyptians. Pharaoh summoned the 'wise men' (Greek, *sophistas*) and sorcerers (Greek, *pharmakous*), those who practice drugging and witchcraft. And the 'charmers' or 'magicians' (*epaoidoi*) did the same things (Exod. 7.11, 22; see also 8.7, 18-19; 9.11).

Hebrew kings sought the services of magicians. Saul 'had expelled the mediums and the wizards from the land' when the Lord did not come to his aid (1 Sam. 28.3-14). Yet he requested the help of a 'medium' (Greek, *engastrimythos*; lit. 'one who has fanciful tales in the belly'). For King Joram and the sorceries of his mother Jezebel see 2 Kgs 9.22; for Manasseh and his augury, soothsayings, sorcery, and dealings with mediums and wizards see 2 Chron. 33.6.

The Hebrew common people also sought help from magicians and others of their sort. Isaiah lists the things that the Lord will remove from Jerusalem and Judah, including the 'skillful magician and expert enchanter' (Isa. 3.1-3). The prophets opposed all such practices as immoral (see, e.g., Isa. 44.25-26; 57.1-3; Jer. 27.9-10; Ezek. 22.28-29; Mic. 5.12; Zech. 10.2). The 'abhorrent practices' of other nations came to be outlawed in the Torah (see Deut. 18.9-11). Those who practiced such abominations were to be put to death (Exod. 22.18; Lev. 19.26, 31; 20.6, 27).

7. See further, A.D. Nock, 'Paul and the Magus', in F.J. Foakes Jackson, K. Lake and H.J. Cadbury (eds.), *The Beginnings of Christianity* (5 vols.; London: Macmillan, 1922–42), V, pp. 164-88.

In New Testament times magicians were artificers who performed 'miracles' and used their artful abilities in dealing with forces of nature, birth, sickness, death, demons, and even love affairs. They used their *mageia* (power or ability) to aid patrons against their enemies. We learn some interesting things about magi from Philostratus's *Life of Apollonius of Tyana*. Apollonius, a wandering sage, miracle worker and Neo-pythagorean philosopher, was once asked by a master, 'What about the Magi?' (*magoi*; Matthew's word). And Apollonius replied, 'They are wise men [*sophoi*] but not in all things' (*Life of Appollonius* 1.26). Merchants were pestered by magi, to whom they often attributed their success in trade or business. However, the merchants' failures were thought to be due to their own thrift or not making sacrifices as often as they should have.

According to Apollonius, lovers are especially addicted to the art of magi, because lovers' sicknesses make them vulnerable. They go to those experts and listen to their quackeries. They accept a box of stones, some coming from forbidden places of the earth, others from the moon and the stars, which they are to wear around their necks. The cheaters take big sums of money from the lovers but do nothing at all to help them. If the treatment succeeds, the art of the magi is praised as sufficient for all things; if it fails, the victim blames himself for something he did not do or forgot to do. Philostratus concludes the subject discussed by saying that he would discourage such arts in order to keep young men from keeping company with magi; they become accustomed to such things, even if only in fun (7.39).

Not all reports about magi are derogatory. Among the upper classes in Roman society magi were associated with the courts of proconsuls and governors. Philo writes:

> True magic is the scientific vision by which the works of nature are discerned in the clearest light. It is thought to be fit for reverence and high praise [μάχητον, lit. 'fought for'], is carefully considered not only by the common people but also by kings and the greatest kings, especially those of the Persians. It is so highly respected that it is said that no one is able to be elevated to the kingship among them without first having become a partner in the order of the Magi (*Spec. Leg*. 3.18).

Philo goes on the say, though, that there is a counterfeit to what he said. It is an evil art pursued by conspicuous beggars, ribald persons and the worst of women and slaves. Magi work with purifications and enchantments, promising by charms and incantations to change love into hatred and hatred into love. Simple and innocent people are deceived by the wiles of magi until the worst misfortunes happen to them, so that friends and family members are silently and gradually destroyed (*Spec. Leg*. 3.18).

Except for Matthew's story of the Magi, *magos* and related words occur in the New Testament elsewhere only in Acts, where Luke gives those who practice magical arts a bad press report. According to Acts 8.9-13, Philip was preaching in the region of Samaria and doing signs (*sēmeia*), such as casting out unclean spirits and healing the paralyzed and lame. A man named Simon 'had practiced magic' (*mageuō*) in the city and amazed the people, 'saying that he was someone great'. They even thought he was the power of God himself, because he amazed them with his magic deeds (*mageia*). But after the people listened to Philip preach about the kingdom of God and the name of Jesus, they were baptized. 'Even Simon himself believed...and was amazed when he saw the signs [*sēmeia*] and great miracles [*dynameis*, 'powers'] that took place'.

Notice that the deeds of Philip are called 'signs' and 'powers', both meaning miracles. Philip was, in other words, performing (doing) miracles. Notice also that Luke does not use those words to describe Simon's acts. Simon was practicing magic (*mageuō*), and his performance was called *mageia*.

Later Peter and John laid their hands on the Samaritan converts, and they received the Holy Spirit. When Simon saw what happened, he offered the apostles money for the power of giving the Spirit by his laying on of hands. Peter replied, 'May your silver perish with you, because you thought you could obtain God's gift with money!' Simon's heart was 'not right before God'. Peter asks him to repent and pray for forgiveness, because he is 'in the gall of bitterness and the chains of wickedness'. Simon asks Peter to pray for him that nothing Peter said might happen to him (Acts 8.14-24).

If Simon the magos was representative of magi and magicians in the first century, then *mageia* was to be condemned, at least according to early Christian standards reported in Acts. In Acts 13.6-12 there is 'a certain magician [*magos*], a Jewish false prophet...with the proconsul, Sergius Paulus', who 'wanted to hear the word of God'. But 'the magician Elymas' tried to persuade the proconsul to turn away from the faith. Paul said to him, 'You son of the devil, you enemy of all righteousness, full of all deceit and villainy, will you not stop making crooked the straight paths of the Lord'? Then Paul adds that Elymas 'will be blind for a while'.[8]

According to Acts 19.11-20, 'God did extraordinary miracles through Paul'. Some 'itinerant Jewish exorcists tried to use the name of the Lord Jesus' to cast out evil spirits as Paul had done. They failed miserably and residents of Ephesus were awestruck. Many who became believers 'confessed and disclosed their practices'. And some of those who practiced magic collected their highly valuable books and 'burned them publicly'. Such books contained the secret formulae used to do 'magic spells' that were revealed to others or copied and sold for a large sum of money. Luke ends the story with a summary of the apostles' work: 'So the word of the Lord grew mightily and prevailed'.

The stories in Acts leave me with some questions. How did Luke distinguish between miracle and magic? What was the difference between the 'signs' and 'powers' performed by Paul and other apostles and the miraculous deeds performed by non-Christians? Was it that the deeds by the apostles were done in the name of Jesus and without hope of personal or financial gain? If the ancients did not separate the phenomenon of magic from that of religion, do the stories in Acts seem to indicate that early Christians began to separate the two phenomena? If so, why? Why did Luke not include a story of the Magi in his birth stories?

According to the stories in Acts, Luke shows no respect at all for magicians and magic. Is that why he left them out of his Gospel? Goulder thinks so. Although Luke means no disrespect to Matthew, his predecessor, 'he cannot have this stuff in his gospel'. Unlike Matthew, whose interests were evil, rich people, Luke 'sanctified both' the poor and disreputable characters. Instead of Matthew's rich Magi Luke has the 'shady' shepherds (see below).[9]

Certainly, the liberation that Christian miracle workers brought to the beneficiaries of their deeds was not liberation from political or socioeconomic oppression, was it? The passages in Acts and what I have said about them, it seems to me, should not be ignored when we consider Matthew's Magi and the liberation he thought Jesus came to bring.

8. For the Magi cf. Horsley, *Liberation*, pp. 53-60. Horsley makes no reference to the passages in Acts, perhaps because they do not fit in with his view of 'the political dimensions' of the star and the Magi.

9. Goulder, *Luke*, I, pp. 248-52.

Flight to Egypt and Return

Matthew reports that after the visit of the wise men Joseph was told by an angel in a dream to 'take the child and his mother, and flee to Egypt, and remain there until I tell you'. One reason for the flight, according to Matthew, is that 'Herod is about to search for the child, to destroy him' (Mt. 2.13). Now that is 'Herod as Herod'! But does that make the incident of the flight more historically trustworthy? Matthew's motive of showing fulfillment of Scripture influenced his telling of the story. The flight to Egypt 'was to fulfill what had been spoken by the Lord through the prophet: "Out of Egypt I have called my son" ' (Mt. 2.15; see also Hos. 11.1). Obviously, if Jesus was to be called out of Egypt so that a prophecy could be fulfilled, he must first have gotten there somehow.

The pericope of the flight to Egypt and the return (Mt. 2.13-21) is marked by symbolism. Herod and Jesus are symbolic of Pharaoh and Moses in Exodus (Exod. 1.15–4.20). Here are some of the parallels between Matthew's story and the account in Exodus. As a baby Moses was saved from death at the hands of the king (Pharaoh) of Egypt by being hidden 'among the reeds on the bank of the river' (Exod. 2.3). As a baby, Jesus was saved from his death planned by Herod by being taken to Egypt in hiding. Moses went to Egypt and then left the country because God told him to. Jesus was taken to Egypt and then left the country because God was responsible for his movements.

Pharaoh is the enemy of Moses and the Israelites. In Matthew's story Archelaus is the enemy of Jesus and the Christians. God tells Moses, 'Go back to Egypt; for all those who were seeking your life are dead' (Exod. 4.19). An angel, speaking for God, tells Joseph in Egypt, 'Take the child … and go to the land of Israel, for those who were seeking the child's life are dead' (Mt. 2.20). 'Moses took his wife and his sons… and went back to the land of Egypt' (Exod. 4.20). 'Joseph…took the child and his mother, and went [back] to the land of Israel' (Mt. 2.21).

According to Matthew, the family of Jesus do not remain in Israel because Herod's son Archelaus was ruling in place of his father. Again, the story rings of probability. But, again, Matthew's primary motive of wanting to get Jesus to Nazareth in Galilee is to fulfill Old Testament Scripture: 'There he made his home in a town called Nazareth, so that what had been spoken through the prophets might be fulfilled, "He will be called a Nazorean" ' (Mt. 2.23).

Weeping for the Dead Children

The lamentation that Matthew implies took place as the result of Herod's murdering of children in and around Bethlehem was to fulfill a prophecy of Jeremiah (Mt. 2.17-18; Jer. 31.15). Matthew's words are very close to those of Jeremiah, which are: 'Rachel is weeping for her children; she refuses to be comforted for her children, because they are no more'. Rachel was the mother of the Joseph tribes of Israel and, according to 1 Sam. 10.2, her tomb was near Ramah.

In Jeremiah the words 'Rachel is weeping for her children' are probably an allusion to some time during the exile of the Israelites, perhaps the deportation of the northern tribes by Assyria after 722–721 BC. The prophet imagined the spirit of Rachel weeping for her children, the deportees. Matthew assumes that as the result of such a vicious deed by Herod there would be misery and lamentation. Although he does not actually report such lamentation, Matthew applies a quotation from Jeremiah to the assumed situation after the time of Herod's act.

There is no evidence whatsoever anywhere else for Herod's murder of the children reported by Matthew. If there were such evidence, Herod would, indeed, have been acting as 'Herod is Herod'. Josephus gives detailed accounts of Herod the Great and his dastardly deeds and the butchery of his relatives, even his own sons and wives, including the wife he loved most. Indeed, Herod had such a bad reputation that the Emperor Augustus supposedly once said it was better to be Herod's pig than his son.[10] The saying was, no doubt, intended to be a pun. The Latin word for pig is *sus*, *suis*, and the word for son is *filius*. The pun is even more pungent in Greek than in Latin. The Greek word for pig is *hus*, and the word for son is *huios*. For this reason the saying may first have been written by a Greek writer and attributed to Augustus. No matter, because of Herod's terrible reputation, even among non-Jews, if he had committed a deed so dastardly that it caused loud lamentation and weeping among Jews (Mt. 2.18), it would not have gone unreported by the Jew Josephus.[11]

10. I do not know the source of this saying, which I have remembered from long ago. Horsley (*Liberation*, p. 178 n. 12) attributes it to the Latin writer Macrobius (AD 400), *Sat.* 2.4.2, but I think it is earlier than that, as what I have just said may indicate.

11. For an account of Herod the man and his work, as well as for Augustus, see Horsley, *Liberation*, pp. 23-52.

There is, however, an interesting parallel to Matthew's story of Herod, Jesus, and the murder of children in Suetonius's life of Augustus. With Herod's question, 'Where is the child who has been born king of the Jews?' (Mt. 2.2) and Herod's murder of the children (Mt. 2.16), compare what Suetonius, quoting another author, says about Augustus:

> A few months before Augustus was born a portent was generally observed at Rome, which gave warning that nature was pregnant with a King for the Roman people. Thereupon the Senate in consternation decreed that no male child born that year should be reared. But those whose wives were with child saw to it that the decree was not filed in the treasury, since each one appropriated the prediction to his own family (*Lives*, 'Augustus' 2.94.3).[12]

The accounts of Matthew and Suetonius have three things in common: a ruler yet to be born to rule over his people, a decree for the murder of children in order to be sure the present regime was not threatened, and the ones for whom the decree was intended were spared, namely, Augustus and Jesus.

Christology in the Stories of Herod and the Wise Men

For Matthew Jesus was the Son of David (Mt. 1.1), who was born to 'save his people from their sins' (Mt. 1.21). As Messiah, Son of David, Jesus was born in Bethlehem of Judea and first worshiped there by the wise men who were not Jews. However, for Matthew Jesus was not only the Son of David; he was also the Son of God: 'Out of Egypt I have called my son' (Mt. 2.15). As God's Son, Matthew believed that Jesus' mission was not restricted to Jews (see especially Mt. 8.29; 14.33; 16.16; 27.40, 43; see also Mt. 26.63; 27.54). For that reason, although he had Jesus return to Israel, the land of the Jews, he did not have Jesus stay there. Rather, he had Jesus go to Galilee, in a town called Nazareth, to fulfill a prophecy that Jesus would be called a Nazorean. But not only that!

As we have learned, Matthew reports that Jesus moved to Capernaum to fulfill a prophecy of Isaiah. In that same passage (Mt. 4.12-16) he refers to Galilee as 'Galilee of the Gentiles' (from Isa. 9.1). Matthew wanted Jesus' move from Judah to Galilee to symbolize the work of Christian missionaries as open to Gentiles as well as to Jews. By con-

12. Trans. from *Suetonius*, LCL, I, p. 265, with punctuation changes.

tinuing to quote from Isaiah—'the people who sat in darkness have seen a great light' (Isa. 9.2; 58.10)—Matthew stresses his view that salvation was available to both Jews and Gentiles.

Galilee as a Feature of Matthew's Vocabulary

Galilee serves as a vital connecting link between the first two chapters of Matthew and the rest of the Gospel. This is especially emphasized by Matthew's statement: 'He went away to the district of Galilee' (Mt. 2.22). It was very appropriate, therefore, for Matthew to have Jesus come 'from Galilee to John at the Jordan, to be baptized by him' (Mt. 3.13).

With the exception of Mk 8.10, the expression 'the district of' occurs nowhere else in the New Testament. However, it is a favorite of Matthew (Mt. 2.22; 15.21; 16.13). The verb translated as 'went away' in the sentence above is *anachōreō*, also a favorite word of Matthew (2.12, 13, 14, 22; 4.12; 9.24; 12.15; 14.13; 15.21; 27.5). With the exception of Mk 3.7 and Jn 6.15, it occurs nowhere else in the Gospels and only in Acts 23.19 and 26.31 elsewhere in the New Testament.

Matthew's special interest in presenting Jesus as the fulfillment of Old Testament prophecy and his special vocabulary with reference to Galilee have influenced his narratives. This already makes them suspect historically, but there are more stylistic features in Matthew's stories.

Other Stylistic Traits in Matthew's Stories

One of the things that make an author's literary style distinctive is his preference for certain words. Below are a few other examples in Matthew.

Mt. 1.18: 'mother'—occurs 26 times in Matthew, including 6 times in the first two chapters, but it occurs only 17 times in each of Mark and Luke. Matthew inserts it 3 times in parallel gospel material where it does not occur.

Mt. 1.19: 'unwilling' (literally, 'not wanting')—'want' occurs 42 times in Matthew, 25 in Mark, 28 in Luke, and is inserted by Matthew 18 times in parallel material.

Mt. 1.19: 'dismiss'—19 in Matthew, 12 in Mark, 15 in Luke, and inserted 8 times.

Mt. 1.19: 'quietly' (or 'secretly')—occurs in Mt. 1.19 and 2.7 but only twice elsewhere in the New Testament.

Mt. 1.20: 'in a dream'—5 in Matthew's stories (1.20; 2.12, 13, 19, 22) and in 27.19 but nowhere else in the New Testament.

Mt. 1.20: 'appear'—13 in Matthew, including 4 in birth stories, 2 in Mark, 2 in Luke, and inserted 5 times.

Mt. 1.20: 'say' (Greek, *legō*)—118 times in Matthew, 36 in Mark, 94 in Luke, and inserted 61 times.

Mt. 1.20: 'take'—16 in Matthew, including 4 in stories, 6 in Mark, 7 in Luke, and inserted 4 times.

These are just a few of many favorite words or expressions used by Matthew that are taken from only a few verses following the genealogy.[13]

J.C. Hawkins[14] lists 'Words and Phrases Characteristic of St Matthew's Gospel'. Of them he says, 'Out of 95 different words and phrases, 25 are found once or more in chapters i,ii... These "characteristic" words and phrases are used considerably more freely in these two chapters than in the rest of the book.'

These examples of stylistic traits of Matthew, along with his special interest in Galilee and in fulfillment quotations, indicate that he has added his own touches to his stories, in spite of whatever sources he may have used.

Summary

A number of sources provided the inspiration for the composition of Matthew's stories of Jesus' birth. Among them are specific Old Testament texts, which he used and altered to serve his purposes. Influence from birth annunciations, appearances of the Lord, stories of the birth and early life of Moses, Samuel, and other Old Testament heroes also played a part in Matthew's work. And not the least important are the theological and christological viewpoints and literary style of Matthew himself. These things make it difficult to tell what materials Matthew acquired from earlier sources and what he added to them. This is particularly true with respect to the annunciation of Mary's conception and the dreams of Joseph that conform so closely to similar phenomena in the Old Testament.

An annunciation to Mary, a virgin, the coming birth, the birth at Bethlehem in the time of Herod, Jesus' residence in Galilee, Jesus as

13. Some of this information is taken from Gundry, *Matthew*, pp. 13-41.

14. *Horae Synopticae* (Grand Rapids: Baker Book House, 1968), pp. 4-10.

Son of God, and the conception through the Holy Spirit all occur also in Luke. Therefore, these items were probably pre-Matthean and pre-Lukan, as most scholars still seem to believe. However, it is likely that, as Goulder thinks, Luke used Matthew as well as Mark in the composition of his stories.

The tradition that Jesus was the Son of God was fixed before Matthew, as we have learned from Paul who writes: 'Jesus Christ...was declared to be Son of God with power according to the spirit of holiness by resurrection from the dead' (Rom. 1.4; see also Acts 13.32-33). Although we cannot be certain here what Paul means, he does associate the spirit (Spirit) with the sonship of Jesus. Matthew, therefore, did not invent the idea of Jesus being Son of God through the Spirit. But by stressing the action of the Spirit in the conception of Jesus and then introducing a quotation from the Old Testament (Hos. 11.1 in Mt. 2.15; see also Num. 23.22; 24.8) to support the idea of Jesus as Son of God, Matthew helps to transfer the inception of Jesus' sonship from the resurrection to his conception and birth (see Lk. 1.32, 35).[15]

15. For some of the topics in this paragraph see Brown, *Birth*, pp. 96-196.

Chapter 6

LUKE'S STORIES OF THE BIRTHS OF JOHN AND JESUS

Luke's Preface (Luke 1.1-4)

We have observed that there is some question about whether Matthew intended the first two words of his Gospel as a title for just the genealogy of Jesus in ch. 1 or for more of the Gospel. In contrast, Luke certainly intended his first four verses to be a formal preface to his whole Gospel and also for his second volume, the book of Acts. We know this for several reasons, but I mention only two. Notice, first of all, that the Gospel of Luke and the book of Acts are addressed to the same person, Theophilus. And notice also that Luke begins Acts by saying, 'In the first book, Theophilus' (Acts 1.1).

When Luke says that 'many have undertaken', his word translated as 'undertaken' (*epecheirēsan*; lit. 'taken in hand') may also be translated as 'attempted'. His word 'many' (*polys*; Mark 61 times; Matthew 60; Luke 60; Acts 67) surely is an exaggeration. Because of Luke's fascination with the word 'many', we do not know how many 'many' was. Goulder remarks that Luke 'was speaking of Mark, Matthew and their predecessors'. Since 'attempted' implies failure, we should use the neutral translation 'have taken in hand' out of consideration for Luke's respect for Mark and Matthew.[1] The word 'attempted' does imply that the authors did not succeed in their attempts. But apparently that is what Luke meant because in Acts 9.29 and 19.13 Luke uses the verb *epicheireō* with precisely that meaning.

At any rate, it appears that Luke was not satisfied with the work of his predecessors, so he decided 'to write accurately in order' (Lk. 1.3, Greek text). The word for 'in order' is *kathexēs*, one not used in the New Testament except by Luke (Lk. 1.3; 8.1; Acts 3.24; 11.4; 18.23),

1. Goulder, *Luke*, I, pp. 198-99.

where sometimes the meaning can be taken as 'in succession'. So if we take Luke's word *kathexēs* in that sense, perhaps Luke was saying that he was writing about events in Jesus' life in the order in which they occurred. This would coincide with his big word *anataxasthai*, meaning 'to put in order' or 'to arrange in order' (Lk. 1.1).

Perhaps Fitzmyer conveys Luke's meaning when he says that Luke intended to write 'a systematic presentation', or as he translates Luke's Greek: 'to put them systematically in writing for you, Theophilus'. However, the idea of 'in succession' seems to be confirmed in Acts. Luke begins Acts by writing: 'In the first book, Theophilus, I wrote about all that Jesus did and taught from the beginning until the day when he was taken up to heaven' (Acts 1.1-2).

The word for 'accurately' is the adverb *akribōs*, used also in Acts 18.25 of Apollos who 'taught accurately the things concerning Jesus'. The noun *akribeia* and the adjective *akribēs* are used in Acts 22.3 and 26.5, where Paul is reportedly speaking about his strict Jewish religious observance. The comparative is used in Acts 18.26 and 24.22, also with reference to greater accuracy about religious matters.

The words mentioned in Acts have religious connotations and indicate that the words in Lk. 1.3 should be taken in the same way. They should not be taken to mean that Luke had done careful research. This is true in spite of the fact that he mentions 'eyewitnesses', because he adds 'and servants of the word', words loaded with theological implications. Moreover, the word translated in the NRSV as 'have been fulfilled' (*plērophoreō*) is a synonym for one used elsewhere by Luke for the fulfillment of Scripture (e.g. Lk. 4.21; 22.37). And the word translated as 'handed on' (*paradidōmi*) was regularly used among early Christians to refer to religious teaching or tradition passed on to others. For example, Paul commends the Christians in the church at Corinth because they 'maintain the traditions just as I handed them on to you' (1 Cor. 11.2; see also 1 Cor. 15.3; Rom. 6.17; Acts 16.4). 'Truth' (*asphaleia*) in Lk. 1.4 originally meant 'physical safety', then 'security' or 'reliability'. Fitzmyer translates it as 'assurance'.[2] These observations indicate that 'the truth' Luke writes about (Lk. 1.4) is more in the nature of religious or theological assurance than historical fact.

2. Fitzmyer, *Gospel*, I, p. 300. He mentions the difficulty of translating *asphaleia* accurately and gives several other possibilities.

Having said only this much about Luke's preface, crucial questions for the historian must remain unanswered. Luke says that 'after investigating everything carefully from the very first', he wrote his account (Lk. 1.3). How could any ancient writer—or even a modern one—possibly investigate *everything*? What records of Jesus' birth were there to be investigated? How can we separate historical facts from interpretation in Luke's account? How did Luke investigate the miraculous incidents he reports? What methods would he have used to investigate them? How would we investigate something taken to be a miracle if we ourselves believed in the actual occurrence of the miracle? If we *believed* it to be a miracle, why would we even try to investigate it? If we thought we had to investigate it, would we actually believe it?

Background for Luke's Stories of Jesus' Birth

Luke's stories of the births of John and Jesus are saturated with knowledge of the Old Testament, and Luke shaped his stories after models taken from it. We have already talked about Luke's use of the Old Testament and observed that the story of Elkanah, Hannah and Samuel probably was the model for much of what Luke writes concerning John and Jesus.[3] Now we consider several other background possibilities.

Story of Abraham and Sarah

There are close parallels between the stories of Abraham and Sarah, Jacob and Rachel, and the parents of Samson and of Samuel and Luke's story of Zechariah, Elizabeth and John. The following are some examples from the story of Abraham and Sarah.

Abraham and Sarah were both very old (Gen. 17.1, 17); so were Zechariah and Elizabeth (Lk. 1.7, 18). The statement about age is repeated in both Genesis and Luke. Sarah was barren (Gen. 11.30), and so was Elizabeth (Lk. 1.7). Of Abraham it is written: 'He kept...my commandments and my regulations' (*tas entolas mou kai ta dikaiōmata mou*; Gen. 26.5). Both Zechariah and Elizabeth lived 'blamelessly (*amemptoi*) according to all the commandments and regulations (*tais entolais kai dikaiōmasin*) of the Lord' (Lk. 1.6). God said to Abraham, 'Be blameless' (*amemptos*; Gen. 17.1). Both Abraham and Zechariah

3. See Goulder, *Luke*, I, pp. 206-18 and parts of pp. 237-54.

want to 'know' some proof that what they hear is to come to pass (Gen. 15.8; Lk. 1.18). The Lord responds to Abraham while in 'a deep sleep' (dream or vision) and reassures him (Gen. 15.12-21). The angel reassures Zechariah while still having his vision (Lk. 1.19-20). When Sarah doubted because of her age, the Lord said to Abraham, 'Shall any word be impossible with God?' (*mē adynatei para tō theō rhēma*; LXX Gen. 18.14). The angel says to Mary concerning Elizabeth: 'No word shall be impossible with God' (*ouk adynatēsei para tou theou pan rhēma*; Lk. 1.37).

Here are some other verbal parallels between the Old Testament story and that of Luke: 'Your wife Sarah shall bear you a son' (Gen. 17.19) and 'Your wife Elizabeth will bear you a son' (Lk. 1.13); 'You shall name him Isaac' (Gen. 17.19) and 'You will name him John' (Lk. 1.13); and 'The child grew' (Gen. 21.8) and 'the child grew' (Lk. 1.80).

Story of Samson

The following are some parallels between Luke's story of John (Lk. 1) and the story of Samson (Judg. 13): 'There was a certain man of Zorah, of the tribe of the Danites, whose name was Manoah' (Judg. 13.2) and 'There was a certain priest whose name was Zechariah, of the priestly order of Abijah' (Lk. 1.5; Greek); 'His wife was barren, having borne no children' (Judg. 13.2) and 'They had no children, because Elizabeth was barren' (Lk. 1.7); 'An angel of the Lord appeared to the woman and said to her' (Judg. 13.3) and 'There appeared to him an angel of the Lord...the angel said to him' (Lk. 1.11, 13); 'Although you are barren...you shall conceive and bear a son' (Judg. 13.3) and 'Elizabeth was barren... Your wife Elizabeth will bear you a son' (Lk. 1.3); 'Now be careful not to drink wine or strong drink' (Judg. 13: 4) and 'He [John] must never drink wine or strong drink' (Lk. 1.15) and 'The boy [Samson] shall be a nazirite [one who abstains from wine and strong drink] to God from birth' (Judg. 13.5), Samson will 'begin to deliver Israel from the hand of the Philistines' (Judg. 13.5) and John 'will turn many of the people of Israel to the Lord their God' (Lk. 1.16); 'The woman bore a son, and named him Samson' (Judg. 13.24) and 'His mother said..."he is to be called John" ' (Lk. 1.60); 'The child grew, and the Lord blessed him' (Judg. 13.24) and 'The child grew and became strong in spirit' (Lk. 1.80); 'The spirit of the Lord began to stir him' (Judg. 13.25) and 'He will be filled with the Holy Spirit even from the womb of his mother' (Lk. 1.15; Greek).

God's Promise to David

The passage in Lk. 1.32-33 has been modeled after the thought and language of several in the Old Testament. With Lk. 1.32-33 compare especially 2 Sam. 7.9-16, God's promise to David made through Nathan the prophet. It became the basis for later Jewish messianic expectation, as we now know from a passage in the Qumran Scrolls (4Q Florilegium 1.10-13). 2 Samuel 7.9-16 reads (Septuagint text):

> I will make you to be named according to the name of the great ones upon the earth. And I will secure a place for my people, for Israel... I will establish his kingdom... I will establish his [David's] throne even forever. I will be to him for a father, and he shall be to me for a son... And his house shall be made sure, and his kingdom forever before me, and his throne shall be set up again forever.

Now look at Lk. 1.32-33 and observe the similarities in language and thought:

> He will be great, and will be called the Son of the Most High, and the Lord God will give to him the throne of his ancestor [Greek, 'father'] David. He will reign over the house of Jacob [Israel] forever, and of his kingdom there will be no end.

It seems certain that Luke was influenced by the passage from 2 Samuel (see also Pss. 2.7; 89.29; Isa. 9.6-7; recall the passage from the *Psalms of Solomon* quoted in Chapter 3). But Jesus the Messiah, according to Luke, is to be not only great, Son of the Most High, have David's throne, and reign over Israel forever in a kingdom without end, but he will also be holy and the Son of God (Lk. 1.32-35).

It is impossible to tell how much of the material in the stories of John and Jesus Luke received from earlier Christian tradition and how much he invented himself on the basis of Old Testament narratives. Perhaps, as some scholars have suggested, there was a longer pre-Lukan source, including Old Testament material, for the story of John from which Luke transferred some things to his story of Jesus. Goulder has suggested that Luke even got the names of Zechariah, Elizabeth and Mary from the Old Testament.[4] However that may be, we can be sure that Luke took bits of information and strands of tradition and wove them creatively into his own account to serve his literary style and theological purposes.

4. Goulder, *Luke*, I, pp. 213-18.

Luke's Literary Style

As with most creative writers, Luke has a literary style of his own. Without becoming too technical, we can observe several interesting things about it.

A special feature of Luke's style in both the Gospel and Acts is the repetition and variation of words and phrases. This is very evident also in the stories of John and Jesus. The passages below are examples of repetition and variation in those stories. Sometimes they occur within the same pericope and sometimes in one pericope and then in another (I translate the same Greek words the same way each time, because that brings out the similarities more accurately): 'Zechariah was troubled' (Lk. 1.12) and Mary 'was greatly troubled' (Lk. 1.29); 'he made signs' (Lk. 1.22) and 'they made signs' (Lk. 1.62); 'he will be called the Son of the Most High' (Lk. 1.32) and 'he will be called the Son of God' (Lk. 1.35); 'the time came for Elizabeth to be delivered' (Lk. 1.57) and 'the time came for her [Mary] to be delivered' (Lk. 2.6); 'her neighbors and relatives' (Lk. 1.58) and 'their neighbors' (Lk. 1.65); 'the neighbors and the relatives' (Lk. 1.58) and 'among their relatives and acquaintances' (Lk. 2.44); and 'they marveled at what was said' (Lk. 2.18) and 'they marveled at what was said' (Lk. 2.33).

Another special feature of Luke's literary style is the way he sometimes distributes and sometimes concentrates closely related words or phrases closely together. The following are some examples of words repeated closely together in Luke's stories of John and Jesus: 'the hill country' (Lk. 1.39, 65); 'redemption' (Lk. 1.68; 2.38); 'make known', (Lk. 2.15, 17); 'the law of the Lord' (Lk. 2.23, 24, 39); and 'rejoicing' (Lk. 1.14, 47, 58).

If you look up the references below, you will see that some repetitions and variations appear in the pericopes about John (Lk. 1.22, 62; 1.58, 65), some in the pericopes about Jesus (Lk. 1.32, 35; 2.15, 17–18; 2.23, 24, 33, 39) and some in the pericopes about John and Jesus (Lk. 1.12, 29; 1.57 and 2.6; 1.39, 65; 1.58 and 2.44; 1.68 and 2.38.

If such variations and repetitions and words and phrases repeated closely together occurred only in Luke's infancy narratives, we might use those stylistic features to argue that Luke used different sources for those narratives than for the rest of his writing. But the literary traits mentioned are characteristic of Luke's writing style in the rest of the Gospel and in Acts.

As with Matthew, favorite words and phrases are a part of Luke's writing style. Here are some examples. 'In the days' (Lk. 1.5, 7, 8) is a favorite phrase, which occurs many times elsewhere in Luke and several times in Acts. Luke likes to begin a sentence with the word *egeneto*, meaning 'it happened' or 'it came to pass', frequently left untranslated, as in the NRSV of Lk. 1.5, 8, for example. Luke prefers to add the word 'name' (*onoma*) with the given name of a person or place, as in Lk. 1.5, 26, 27; 2.25. Luke prefers either *eipon* or *eipen* for the verb 'say' instead of *legō*, Matthew's favorite. A special favorite of Luke's is *tis*, 'a certain', for example, 'a certain priest' (Lk. 1.5). It is left untranslated there and often elsewhere in the NRSV.

The word for until (*achri*) in Lk. 1.20 is a favorite, which occurs 4 times in Luke and 15 times in Acts but only once each in Mark and Matthew. Luke often writes about feelings of joy or happiness, as in Lk. 1.28 (*chairō*), 1.44 (*agalliasis*) and 2.10 (*chara*). The three words for joy are favorites. The first occurs 12 times in Luke, 2 in Mark, and 6 in Matthew; the second, twice in Luke, once in Acts, but nowhere in Mark or Matthew; the third, 12 times in Luke–Acts, once in Mark and 6 times in Matthew.[5]

These few statistics help to inform us about Luke's peculiar literary style. Earlier I mentioned a scholar by the name of (to use Luke's diction) John C. Hawkins. He lists 151 words and phrases characteristic of Luke's Gospel, and then he says that of them 'no less than 77, being more than half of them, occur once or more in chapters i, ii...and there are no less than 115 of them in Acts... We find here (as in the case of Matthew, but not to so large an extent) that such expressions are used more abundantly in the first two chapters than in the rest of the gospel.'[6]

This information indicates how Luke used his own peculiar literary style in writing the various pericopes of his stories about John and Jesus. Keeping in mind the stylistic features of Luke just illustrated, study carefully the table below on the annunciation and birth of John and of Jesus. You will observe some more of the kinds of examples I have listed. But it is important to observe that in spite of the many similarities between the stories of John and Jesus, there are also many subtle differences in the way Luke writes about his two protagonists. I shall say more about this point later.

5. For other Lukan special vocabulary see Goulder, *Luke*, I, pp. 218-20, 233-37, 244-46, 253-55, 261-64, 268-69, 272-73, 279-81, 290-91, *et al.*

6. Hawkins, *Horae Synopticae*, pp. 16-25.

Parallels in the Birth Stories

John	*Jesus*
Birth occurs in time of Herod	Birth occurs in time of Herod
Zechariah has wife whose name was Elizabeth	Mary engaged to a man whose name was Joseph
Conception of John miraculous	Conception of Jesus miraculous
Parents were old and Elizabeth was barren	Mary was a virgin and had not had sexual intercourse
Angel of the Lord appeared to Zechariah	Angel Gabriel sent by God to the virgin
Zechariah was troubled at seeing angel	Mary was greatly troubled by Gabriel's words
Angel says, Do not be afraid, Zechariah	Angel says, Do not be afraid, Mary
Zechariah's prayer has been heard by God	Mary has found favor with God
Elizabeth will bear you a son	You will conceive and bear a a son
You will name him John	You will name him Jesus
His name is John	He was called Jesus
Zechariah said, How will I know this? For I am an old old man	Mary said, How can this be, since I do not know a man?
Zechariah will become mute, unable to speak	Joseph never utters a word
Conception was natural through human sexual relations	Conception was supernatural; Mary did not 'know' a man for sexual relations
Conception like those of special persons in the Old Testament	Conception unique: Holy Spirit will come upon Mary
Zechariah told: He will be great in the sight of the Lord; will be called the prophet of the Most High and filled with the Holy Spirit	Mary told: He will be great and will be called the Son of the Most High; will be called holy, the Son of God
He will turn many of the people of Israel to the Lord their God	The Lord God will give to him the throne of his ancestor David
With the spirit and power of Elijah…to make ready a people prepared for the Lord	He will reign over the house of Jacob forever, and of his kingdom there will be no end
The Lord has … looked favorably on me	The Lord has looked with favor on…his servant

John	*Jesus*
When Elizabeth heard Mary's greeting, the child leaped in her womb	Mary greeted Elizabeth
Elizabeth was filled with the Holy Spirit	The Holy Spirit will come upon you
Elizabeth said, Blessed are you among women	Mary said, From now on all generations will call me blessed
Elizabeth wonders why the mother of my Lord should come to me	Mary inspired to utter the Magnificat
Many will rejoice at his birth	My spirit rejoices in God my Savior
The time was fulfilled for Elizabeth to give birth	The days were fulfilled for her to give birth
And she bore a son	She gave birth to her son
At his birth the neighbors and relatives rejoiced with Elizabeth because the Lord had shown great mercy to her	At his birth an angel announced to the shepherds, I am bringing you good news of great joy for all the people
Her neighbors and relatives	Their relatives and friends
Zechariah said, The Lord God looked favorably on his people and redeemed them. He has raised up a mighty savior for us in the house of his servant David	Angel said, To you is born this day in the city of David a Savior, who is the Messiah, the Lord
That we would be saved from our enemies	My eyes have seen your salvation, which you have prepared in the presence of all peoples
You will go before the Lord to prepare his ways	
To give knowledge of salvation to his people	For the glory of your people Israel
To give light to those who sit in darkness	A light for revelation to the Gentiles
The child grew and became strong in spirit	The child grew and became strong, filled with wisdom; and the favor of God was upon him
John was in the wilderness until the day he appeared publicly to Israel	At 12 Jesus was in his Father's house manifesting his wisdom

We have observed earlier how Luke subtly blends material from the Old Testament in with his stories about John and Jesus. Now this table helps us to observe that Luke also interweaves material about the two characters John and Jesus together in separate pericopes about each of them.

Other Lukan Features in his Birth Stories

As we have already observed, 'Most High', a metonym for God found frequently in the Hebrew scriptures, occurs most often in Luke's writings. In addition to the birth stories see Lk. 6.35 and Acts 7.48. Luke uses 'Son of the Most High God' in Lk. 8.28 (from Mk 5.7, its only occurrence in Mark) and 'the Most High God' in Acts 16.17 (see also Acts 7.48). Matthew, certainly a Jewish writer, does not use 'Most High' for God at all.

In the infancy narratives there are several other phenomena characteristic of Lukan writings. First, in addition to those narratives Luke mentions the appearance of angels in the body of the Gospel (Lk. 22.43; 24.23) and frequently in Acts (e.g. Acts 5.19; 7.30, 35, 38; 8.26; 10.3, 7; 12.7; 27.23). Except for the infancy narratives, Matthew does not mention an appearance of an angel in the same way Luke does (see Mt. 28.2, 5). And Mark mentions such an appearance only in Mk 1.13.

One of Luke's special interests is the Spirit or the Holy Spirit. According to Luke in both his Gospel and Acts, the Spirit itself acts and motivates people to speak and act (e.g. Lk. 2.25-27; Acts 2.4; 8.29-30, 39; 11.12). Luke speaks of the Holy Spirit coming upon persons in Lk. 1.35 and Acts 1.8. And the expression 'filled with the Holy Spirit' is peculiar to Luke in the New Testament (Lk. 1.15, 41, 67; Acts 2.4; 4.8, 31; 9.17; 13.9). The Davidic Messiah in Lk. 1.32-33 becomes specifically the Christian Messiah through the power of the Holy Spirit that made it possible for Mary as a virgin to conceive Jesus (Lk. 1.35).

There is no parallel in the Old Testament to the concept of the Holy Spirit coming upon the person who is to give birth to the messianic ruler. However, 'the Spirit of the Lord will rest upon' the branch from the stump of Jesse (Isa. 11.1-2), that is, the messianic ruler himself. And 'whoever is left in Zion and remains in Jerusalem will be called holy' at the time of 'the branch of the Lord', that is, the Messiah (Isa. 4.2-6). Compare 'the child [Jesus] to be born will be holy' (Lk. 1.35).

Summaries such as those in Lk. 1.80; 2.40; and 2.52 are a characteristic feature of Luke's literary style, not only in the infancy narratives but also in the Gospel and Acts. Luke 4.14-15, for example, gives a glowing summary of Jesus' work: 'Then Jesus, filled with the power of the Spirit, returned to Galilee, and a report about him spread through all the surrounding country. He began to teach in their synagogues and was praised by every one.'

The summary in Lk. 2.52—'And Jesus increased in wisdom and in stature and in favor with God and humans' (my trans.)—ties the last two sections of the infancy narratives in with what precedes and with the body of the Gospel that follows. The favor of Jesus with God has already been demonstrated by Luke, beginning with Jesus' conception and continuing through his youth. Jesus' favor with humans is demonstrated after he makes his first public speech: 'All spoke well of him and were amazed at the gracious words that came from his mouth' (Lk. 4.22; see also Lk. 4.37; 7.17; Acts 2.41-47; 4.32-35; 5.11-16; 6.7; 9.31; 12.24; 16.5; 19.20; 28.30-31).

Date of Jesus' Birth

In the stories of Jesus' birth neither Matthew nor Luke mentions the actual date Jesus was born, nor is a date for that event mentioned anywhere else in the New Testament. So how do we know when Jesus was born? We really do not know for sure, but if we want to determine the time of his birth as accurately as we can, we must try to fix that event at a time that coincides with contemporary events or persons whose dates are reasonably certain.

Jesus was a Jew, Christianity originated within Judaism, and for decades Christianity did not exist apart from Judaism. But Christianity eventually became separated from Judaism, and since then the two religions have existed simultaneously. For that reason some Jewish and Christian scholars today use the designation 'the common era' (Jewish–Christian) for time after the birth of Jesus. Therefore, instead of using BC ('before Christ') and AD (*anno Domini*, 'in the year of the Lord', or 'after Christ'), those scholars use BCE ('before the common era') and CE ('the common era'), particularly when referring to biblical events. In that way the Christian bias in using the designations BC and AD is avoided. From here on in this work I shall use the designations BCE and CE.

Christians did not become concerned about developing a calendar of their own until several centuries after the birth of Jesus. Then they first tried to fix dates for events in his life. First of all, they tried to establish a date for the last Passover of Jesus with his disciples (see Mk 14.12-25; Mt. 26.17-29; Lk. 22.7-23). They did this, of course, because they wanted to determine the date of Easter (the celebration of Jesus' resurrection), which became the most important Christian festival.

As time went on, Christians also became interested in fixing the time of Jesus' birth, and to do that they tried to establish the date of Herod's death, since he died soon after Jesus was born. However, that was not an easy task for several reasons. First of all, Jews reckoned dates from the time of the creation of the world, which they thought occurred at a time that corresponds with our date of 3761 BCE. But Christians wanted to date their festivals from the time of Jesus' birth. Second, Christians did not have access to published and official calendars like those today. And third, Romans dated events from the time of the founding of the city of Rome (*ab urbe condita* [*a.u.c.*], 'from the founding of the city').

By the sixth century CE Christians began fixing dates for Jesus' birth and his resurrection. Perhaps it was the Roman monk Dionysius Exiguus (called 'Dennis the Little') who thought Herod the Great died in 754 *a.u.c.* Because there is no date zero BCE or CE, Herod's death would have occurred in the last year before Jesus was born or 1 BCE, as now designated. However, later someone else fixed the date of Herod's death at 750 *a.u.c.* which corresponds with 4 BCE. So, if we allow two years for Herod's decree for the death of 'all the children in and around Bethlehem who were two years old or under' (Mt. 2.16) to be effective, we have the time of 6–4 BCE as the most likely date of Jesus' birth.

Besides Herod the Great several other persons, whose chronological dates are reasonably certain, are mentioned in the stories of Jesus' birth or elsewhere in the Gospels. In his introduction to the preaching of John the Baptist Luke says, 'In the fifteenth year of the reign of Emperor Tiberius...the word of God came to John son of Zechariah in the wilderness' (Lk. 3.1-2). Tiberius was the second emperor of Rome and ruled from 14–37 CE. According to Luke, therefore, this would mean that John began his public work about 28–29 CE. Since Jesus was only six months younger than John (see Lk. 1.26), presumably Jesus also began his public life about the same time, or about 29–30 CE. This presumption is supported by Luke's statement that 'Jesus was about thirty years old when he began his work' (Lk. 3.23).

According to the evidence just considered, Jesus would have been born about 1 BCE or 1 CE, because there is no theoretical zero year between the time reckoned BCE and CE. Since for about 15 centuries dates have been reckoned from the time of Jesus' birth, the usual belief is that Jesus was born about 1 CE. But if we consider further evidence, fixing the year Jesus was born becomes more complicated.

Both Matthew and Luke mention a Herod as king at the time of

Jesus' birth. Matthew says that the wise men came to see Jesus 'in the time of King Herod' (Mt. 2.1). And Luke writes: 'In the days of King Herod of Judea, there was a priest named Zechariah' (Lk. 1.5). The Herod mentioned was Herod the Great, who ruled as King of Judea, the land of the Jews, for Rome from 37–34 BCE, the year of his death. If we had only that information, it would be simple to fix the date of Jesus' birth sometime close to 4 BCE, since Jesus was born shortly before Herod died. We know this because Herod's son Archelaus (4 BCE–6 CE) was already ruling in the place of Herod when Joseph brought the child Jesus back to Israel from Egypt (Mt. 2.21-22).

If Herod's decree for the death of 'all the children in and around Bethlehem who were two years old or under' (Mt. 2.16) was issued the year he died (4 BCE), it would mean that Jesus would surely be killed if born after 6 BCE. The date for the birth of Jesus would, then, be sometime between about 6–4 BCE. However, the problem becomes even more complicated when we take Luke's story into further account.

In Lk. 2.1 we read: 'A decree went out from Emperor Augustus that all the world should be registered...while Quirinius was governor of Syria'. Since Herod ruled from 37–34 BCE. and Augustus from 27 BCE–14 CE, Jesus' birth certainly fell within the timespan of their reigns. So there is no difficulty in reconciling the date of Jesus' birth with the reigns of Herod and Augustus. The problems arise with the registration, which included 'all the world', and its occurrence during the time of Quirinius of Syria.

Rome sometimes did take a census in certain parts of her empire. Such a census was always taken, though, for the purpose of taxation and never included 'all the world', that is, the whole Roman Empire. Josephus mentions a census taken at the deposition of Archelaus in 6 CE, but it was limited to Judea and, therefore, did not include Galilee, where the hometown of Joseph and Mary was located. Josephus writes: 'Quirinius went to Judea for the purpose of evaluating the possessions of the residents [including Jews, of course] and selling the property of Archelaus' (*Ant.* 18.1.1).

As with Augustus, Quirinius was a historical character whose existence is attested by persons other than Luke. However, the best evidence by far indicates that he became governor of Syria in 6 or 7 CE. Although it has been argued that Quirinius was governor of Syria about 3 BCE, as well as in 6 or 7 CE, the evidence for that calculation in order to make Luke's story historical is too dubious to consider.

There were Roman censuses at times other than the one during the time of Quirinius, but we cannot fit Luke's story in with any of them. We know of no census conducted in the way Luke describes it. Joseph would have been registered in his hometown Nazareth, not in the town where his ancestors had lived several hundred years earlier. Remember that Luke says Joseph and Mary 'returned to Galilee, to their own town of Nazareth' (Lk. 2.39).

In sum, Matthew and Luke agree in fixing the time of Jesus' birth before the death of Herod in 4 BCE. Perhaps, then, Jesus was born sometime between 6–4 BCE. It seems quite likely, therefore, that Luke used the census by Quirinius and Joseph's trip to Bethlehem as literary devices to locate the place of Jesus' birth at Bethlehem in accordance with earlier Christian tradition.

According to Horsley, the census is more than 'a purely literary device' and more than the resolution of a christological problem. Luke thought of Jesus as opposing Roman taxation, which was a symbol of domination, subjection and exploitation. The juxtaposition of an imperial decree with Jesus' birth 'is the height of political-economic-religious conflict: the messiah now being born would lead the people's successful resistance against that false and intolerable lordship and subjection'.[7] Here Horsley does not object to finding symbolism in what Luke says. In spite of that, his view is a credible alternative to the one of the census as a literary device. However, a good case can be made for Luke's Messiah as a bringer of peace, not military conquest (see below).

Before moving on to another subject we should note one fact, that is, that Luke does not always get his facts straight. He is mistaken about the date of the census by Quirinius by placing it at the time of Jesus' birth. In the same way, Luke places the uprising of Theudas in the time of the procurator Fadus (44–46 CE) before the census in the time of Judas the Galilean (6 CE; see Acts 5.36-37 and Josephus, *Ant.* 20.5.1).

It should be noted here also that Luke's reference to 'the city of David called Bethlehem', a phrase that occurs only in Lk. 2.4 (see also 'city of David' in Lk. 1.11) in the New Testament, is also in error. Although the phrase 'city of David' occurs in both the Hebrew and Greek Old Testament, it always refers to the city of Jerusalem, more specifically to the 'stronghold of Zion' (see, e.g., 2 Sam. 5.7, 9; 6.10,

7. Horsley, *Liberation*, pp. 34-38.

12, 16; 1 Kgs 8.1; 11.27). The word for 'city' in 'city of David' is always *polis*, not *kōmē*, 'village', as in Jn 7.42: 'the Messiah comes from Bethlehem, the village where David was from' (my trans.).

It appears that the author of the fourth Gospel was correcting Luke by changing *polis* to *kōmē* and saying 'Bethlehem where David was from'. This avoids Luke's incorrect terminology of Bethlehem as the 'city of David' by referring to Bethlehem only as the village where David resided. Jerusalem could not, then, be thought of as the place of the Messiah's birth, and the specifically Christian tradition that the Messiah was to be born in Bethlehem is upheld.

Goulder thinks that Luke's memory of the census in Galilee during the time of Judas the Galilean (Acts 5.37) gave Luke the idea for the one at the time of Jesus' birth. Luke knew that Roman officials 'did not tour every farm' but expected people to sign up at local towns. As a descendant of David, Joseph had to go to Bethlehem for the census, dignified by Luke into a worldwide one. Luke's error 'of a decade may seem a peccadillo'.[8]

Brown calls attention to various motives of Luke with respect to the census and the shifting of the scene for Jesus' birth from Galilee to Bethlehem. Brown opts for the census of Israel and Judah decreed by David in 2 Samuel 24 as the background for Luke's census.[9]

According to Matthew, the Bethlehem tradition arose from the motive of fulfilling Old Testament prophecy. I think that Luke's story of the census and the trip to Bethlehem is a literary device to get Mary to Bethlehem for the birth of her son in keeping with the legend of his birth there. Fitzmyer's neutral explanation avoids both the idea of a literary device and the problem of history for the census. According to Fitzmyer, Luke was not thinking in terms of 'historical detail. His purpose is to get Mary (who is with child) to Bethlehem in time for the birth of Jesus there.'[10] But the mention of Bethlehem still leaves us with a historical problem precisely because it was not one for Luke.

8. Goulder, *Luke*, I, pp. 249-51.
9. Brown, *Birth*, pp. 412-18.
10. Fitzmyer, *Gospel*, I, p. 406.

Chapter 7

LUKE'S PORTRAYAL OF JOHN AND OF JESUS

Why does only Luke use narratives about John, along with those of Jesus, to serve as an introduction to his Gospel? From a literary point of view, Luke ties the stories of John in ch. 1 in with the body of the Gospel in several ways. Luke concludes his story of the annunciation and birth of John by saying, 'He was in the wilderness until the day he appeared publicly to Israel' (Lk. 1.80). Then after listing the rulers of Palestine and the territories over which they ruled in the time of the Emperor Tiberius, Luke brings John on the scene by saying: 'The word of God came to John son of Zechariah in the wilderness' (Lk. 3.2). Only Luke refers to John as the son of Zechariah. And Luke generally prefers the simple name John (Lk. 3.15, 20; 7.28; 9.7; Acts 10.37; 11.16; 13.24) without further description. He rarely adds descriptive titles such as 'the baptizer' (*ho baptizōn*; Mk 1.4; 6.14, 24) or 'the baptist' (*ho baptistēs*; Mt. 3.1; 11.11; 14.2, 8; but see Lk. 7.20, 33; 9.19).

The Parents of the Boys

We have observed that Luke's literary interests play a prominent part in the composition of his birth stories. There is also a strong christological motive behind what he says about John and his parents and how he says it. Although Luke believed both John and Jesus were agents in God's plan for the salvation of humankind, Luke presents his story in a way that shows Jesus as superior to John. The child in Elizabeth's womb already leaped for joy when Mary greeted Elizabeth. Elizabeth questioned why the mother of her Lord should come to her. Luke makes it clear that already before Jesus' birth Jesus, not John, is to be Lord (Lk. 1.41-44).

Luke also portrays Jesus' parents as superior to those of John. The conception of John was miraculous because both Zechariah and Elizabeth were beyond the childbearing age, and Elizabeth was barren. We assume, of course, that Elizabeth conceived naturally through sexual intercourse. The conception of Mary was also miraculous, but it was even more miraculous than Elizabeth's. It happened, without sexual relations, through the Holy Spirit that came upon Mary as a virgin so that she conceived.

There is another big difference, a curious one, though, with respect to the two sets of parents. Matthew says that Mary's husband Joseph was 'a righteous man' (Mt. 1.19). However, Matthew says nothing about Mary being righteous, unless, of course, a righteous status is assumed because she was a virgin. With respect to the parents of John, Luke says, 'Both of them were righteous before God, living blamelessly according to all the commandments and regulations of the Lord' (Lk. 1.6). Luke says nothing about Mary living in accordance with the laws of God. On the other hand, Luke never mentions that Joseph was a righteous man. And, like Matthew, Luke does not say that Mary was righteous, unless, again, we assume such a status because she was a virgin. How can we explain these differences?

Were the differences due to Mary's ill repute in some Jewish circles? Would Luke not have wanted to call Joseph righteous because he married Mary? For Matthew, of course, the righteous Joseph represents the usual Jewish reaction to the pregnancy of Mary before marriage. However, Joseph's acceptance of Mary as a virtuous woman because of Isaiah's prophecy helps to acquit her of guilt in the eyes of Matthew's critics.

The Boys about to Be Born

Luke cleverly portrays a progression in the physical and spiritual development of Jesus compared with that of John. As a child, John 'grew and became strong in spirit' (Lk. 1.80). The boy Jesus was presented to the Lord, and he was recognized as 'the Lord's Messiah' (Lk. 2.22-26). In contrast to John, the child Jesus not only 'grew and became strong' but also was 'filled with wisdom; and the favor of God was upon him' (Lk. 2.40; see LXX Gen. 21.8; Judg. 13.24; 1 Sam. 2.21, 26; Isa. 11.2). With Lk. 2.40 and 2.52 see *Pss. Sol.* 17.37, written about the Messiah to come: 'God will make him...wise by means of the spirit of understanding'.

In contrast to John, who went off to live in the wilderness, Jesus went with his parents to the Passover at Jerusalem. There he not only demonstrated his precocity but also acknowledged God as his Father. Jesus is thus given more publicity than John. Moreover, Jesus is also shown to be superior in growing up. And the second summary of Jesus' growth shows a progression in Jesus' own development over that in the first summary (Lk. 2.40): 'And Jesus increased in wisdom and in stature [i.e. in age and size], and in favor with God and humans' (Lk. 2.52; my trans.).

There is also an important contrast in the attributes and work predicted for the two men, as the following passages show.

John	*Jesus*
will be great in the sight of the Lord and be called the prophet of the Most High (Lk. 1.15, 76).	will be great, and will be called the Son of the Most High... and will be holy...called Son of God (Lk. 1.32, 35).
The Lord God of Israel...has looked favorably on his people and redeemed them (Lk. 1.68).	is born a Savior, who is the Messiah, the Lord (Lk. 2.11).
will turn many of the people of Israel to the Lord their God...and give knowledge of salvation to his people by the forgiveness of their sins (Lk. 1.16, 77).	Simeon has seen God's salvation... prepared in the presence of all peoples, a light for revelation to the Gentiles and for glory to your people Israel (Lk. 2.29-32).

In the passages that praise John the emphasis is on his work among the Jews. God has redeemed '*his* people', 'people of Israel', salvation to 'his [God's] people' and the forgiveness of 'their sins'. In contrast to the work of John, Jesus comes as 'a Savior', whose work of salvation is for 'all peoples' and a revelation 'to the Gentiles'. Observe that in the last passage quoted Luke places 'the Gentiles' before 'your people Israel' (see below). And most significant is the fact that God is the one who brings salvation through his agent John. Conversely, Jesus himself is 'a Savior, who is the Messiah, the Lord' (Lk. 2.11). And in the words of Simeon, who has just seen Jesus and speaks about him, Jesus is God's 'salvation...prepared in the presence of all peoples' (Lk. 2.30-31).

John and Jesus in God's Plan

It is generally recognized that throughout his Gospel Luke has a special interest in non-Jews as the beneficiaries of Jesus' work. Luke seems to think of at least two, if not three, eras in God's plan for the salvation of the human race. In typical fashion, Luke repeats the theme with linguistic variations. First, in her Magnificat Mary proclaims: 'He [the Lord] has helped his servant Israel, in remembrance of his mercy, according to the promise he made to our ancestors, to Abraham and to his descendants forever' (Lk. 1.54-55).

Second, Zechariah speaks his prophecy: 'Blessed be the Lord God of Israel, for he has looked favorably on his people and redeemed them... He has shown the mercy promised to our ancestors, and has remembered his holy covenant, the oath that he swore to our ancestor Abraham' (Lk. 1.68, 72-73).

According to Luke, the birth of John marked the end of the first era in God's plan for the salvation of humankind that began with Abraham. John fulfilled God's plan for the salvation of the Jews up to his own time. The verbs in the passages quoted are all in the past tense. Through John God has kept his promises to his people. But John also was the forerunner of Jesus, whose birth signaled the beginning of the second era. Jesus is to continue John's work and go beyond John. Jesus is Savior/Messiah/Lord, God's salvation, 'prepared in the presence of all peoples, a light for revelation to the Gentiles and for glory to your people Israel' (Lk. 2.30-32).

For Gentiles and Israel

With respect to Lk. 2.32, the crucial question is: Did or did not Luke mean to show priority to the Gentiles in God's bestowing of salvation 'prepared in the presence of all peoples' by placing Gentiles before Israel? 'Salvation' in 2.30 becomes a 'light' in 2.32. Here Luke was influenced by texts from Isaiah. See, for example, LXX Isa. 49.6: 'I have given you [the Lord's servant] for a covenant of a race, for a light of Gentiles, that you should be for salvation to the end of the earth' (see also Isa. 42.6). Consider also LXX Isa. 60.1, 3: 'Your light has come [upon Jerusalem], and the glory of the Lord has risen upon you... And kings shall walk in your light, and Gentiles in your brightness.'

In the last passage light and glory are in apposition and in the same sequence as they are in Lk. 2.32. And Gentiles shall benefit from the light, also as in Luke. But the priority is with the Jews, as it is also in Isa. 49.6. So the passages from Isaiah do not give us any help for solving the priority question in Lk. 2.32.

Fitzmyer seems to favor the priority of Israel and, along with other scholars, points to Paul as sharing the same idea. Consider, for example, Rom. 1.16: 'for salvation to everyone who has faith, to the Jew first and also to the Greek' (see also Rom. 2.10).[1] Horsley leaves no doubt about Fitzmyer's understanding: Simeon's song appears 'to give Israel a clear priority'. While the Gentiles are beneficiaries, 'God's salvation is focused on—indeed is—the redemption of Israel'.[2] Horsley is wrong, as we shall see. Brown's position is in the middle: 'Revelation for the Gentiles and glory for Israel are two equal aspects of the one salvation and light that God has made ready. Neither is subordinate to the other.'[3] It appears that Brown is also wrong.

Once again Luke himself helps us solve the problem at hand. See Acts 4.27: 'with the Gentiles and the peoples of Israel'. According to Acts 9.15, the Lord told Ananias that he has chosen Paul as an instrument 'to bring my name before Gentiles and kings and before the people of Israel' (see Isa. 60.1, 3 quoted above). The same priority, Gentiles and Jews, is found also in Acts 13.46; 14.5; 15.14-19. However, there is an exception, as with every rule, in Acts 26.23.

In Acts 26.23 Paul is making his defense before King Agrippa II: that Agrippa was a great-grandson of Herod the Great; and, like Herod, he had some Jewish blood in his veins. But whether because of his partly Jewish heritage he was 'especially familiar with all the customs and controversies of the Jews' (Acts 26.3), as Paul reportedly said, is debatable. Nevertheless, Agrippa undoubtedly did help the cause of the Jews and Judaism. At great cost, he imported lumber from Lebanon for the repair of the temple of the Jews in Jerusalem. And he and his sister Bernice (see Acts 25.13, 23; 26.30) did all they could to prevent an all-out war of the Jews against Rome in 66 CE.

Whether Agrippa was motivated by his own convictions about Judaism or the desire for personal political gain or both is also debatable. At any rate, it was highly appropriate for Luke to have Paul, while making his defense before Agrippa, not only to remark about Agrippa's expertise on Judaism, but also to have Paul say on that special occasion that the Messiah would 'proclaim light both to our people [the Jews] and to the Gentiles' (Acts 26.23). In putting the Jews first in Paul's speech before Agrippa Luke was only being diplomatic. In light of what I have just said, it is easy to understand why Acts 26.23 is the exception that makes the rule, and that in Lk. 2.32, as elsewhere in Acts, priority for the Gentiles is intended.

1. Fitzmyer, *Gospel*, I, p. 428.
2. Horsley, *Liberation*, p. 120.
3. Brown, *Birth*, p. 440.

Early in his Gospel Luke reports that Jesus was recognized as 'the Holy One of God' (Lk. 4.34, from Mk 1.24), 'the Son of God' and 'the Messiah' (Lk. 4.41, a passage only in Luke). Thus, the promises made concerning the sonship, holiness and messiahship of Jesus in the stories of his birth (Lk. 1.32, 35; 2.26) are fulfilled. According to Luke, Jesus was quickly recognized as unique and became so popular that 'the crowds...wanted to prevent him from leaving them. But he said to them, "I must proclaim the good news of the kingdom of God to the other cities also; for I was sent for this purpose" ' (Lk. 4.42-43).

The verb translated as 'proclaim the good news' is a single Greek word, *euangelizō*, one of Luke's favorites (10 times in Luke, 15 in Acts, 1 in Matthew, 0 in Mark). It ties the preceding stories in nicely with Jesus' reading from Isa. 61.1-2 and applying it to himself while in the synagogue at Nazareth (Luke 4.16-21). *Euangelizō* also ties in the narratives in Lk. 4.14-43 with the 'good news' announced to Zechariah about John (Lk. 1.19) and the 'good news of great joy for all the people' proclaimed by the angel to the shepherds at the birth of Jesus (Lk. 2.10).

The two eras in God's plan for the salvation of humankind, according to Luke, are clearly stated in Lk. 16.16: 'The law and the prophets were in effect until John came; since then the good news [*euangelizō*] of the kingdom of God is proclaimed'. Recall here the words of Jesus about proclaiming the kingdom of God (Lk. 4.42-43) quoted above. The second era was greater than the first, according to Luke, because Jesus was greater than John.

Luke had already found a not-too-subtle subordination of John to Jesus in his sources, the Gospel of Mark and Q. This seems to indicate that there was some competition, if not controversy, between the followers of John the Baptist and Jesus.

John and Jesus in the Synoptic Gospels

We know little historically about the Baptist and his relationship with Jesus. Only Luke mentions that their mothers were relatives (Lk. 1.36). So, according to Luke, John would be related to Jesus. However, if John and Jesus ever met depends on whether we accept Jesus' baptism by John as a historical fact, a question we need not discuss.

In the Role of Elijah

There is one significant difference between what Luke says about John with respect to Elijah in the stories of John's infancy and in the body of his Gospel. In the last of the Old Testament prophets, Malachi, there are two predictions about persons to come before the last days. The one prophecy is: 'Behold, I am sending out my messenger, and he will look out [Greek, *epiblepō*] a way before me, and the Lord whom you are looking for will suddenly come to his temple' (LXX Mal. 3.1). The other prediction is: 'Behold, I am sending you the prophet Elijah before the great and manifest day of the Lord comes' (LXX Mal. 3.23; Heb. 4.5-6; see also Sir. 48.10).

In early Christian tradition Mal. 3.1 was combined with Isa. 40.3 and applied to the Baptist. This was done in Mk 1.2-3: 'See, I am sending my messenger ahead of you, who will prepare [Greek, *kataskeuazō*] your way; the voice of one crying out in the wilderness: "Prepare [Greek, *hetoimazō*] the way of the Lord, make his paths straight" '. Although Mark attributes the whole quotation to Isaiah, the first part is from Mal. 3.1. Matthew and Luke both retain the quotation from Isa. 40.3 but omit the part from Malachi. Luke continues the quotation from Isa. 40.3-5 far enough to include the words (from the LXX): 'and all flesh shall see the salvation of God'. Words for salvation are favorites of Luke and occur six times in the Gospel (four in birth stories), seven in Acts, once in Mark, and not at all in Matthew.

In Lk. 7.27 Luke does quote Mal. 3.1, and it is the only passage in the body of the Gospel whereby the Baptist is put in the role of Elijah. Thus, it coincides with Lk. 1.17, where John is to be the one who will go before Jesus 'with the spirit and power of Elijah...to turn the hearts of parents to their children...to make ready a people prepared for the Lord' (from Mal. 3.23). But elsewhere in Luke Jesus is compared with Elijah (Lk. 4.25-30; see also Lk. 9.54 and 2 Kgs 1.9-14). Luke omits the passage in Mk 9.9-13 [retained in Mt. 17.9-13], where Jesus is reported as saying that Elijah has come 'and they did to him [the Baptist] whatever they pleased'.

In order to alleviate the problem, Brown suggests that Luke may reflect two stages in Christian thinking about Elijah. An earlier stage is reflected in Luke's account of Jesus' work where Jesus is identified as the eschatological prophet of the end times like Elijah (Lk. 7.16). A later stage, perhaps composed after the Gospel and Acts were written, is dominant in Luke's infancy stories and stresses Jesus as Son of God.

According to Brown, that kind of shift would leave Elijah for the role of the Baptist, a role only hinted at in the Gospel account but made clear in the infancy story. But ultimately Brown concludes that everything in Lk. 1.13-17 'is consonant with' what Luke says of the Baptist in Lk. 3.1-20 and 7.18-35.[4] However, for persons not satisfied with such a solution, the problem of the differences between the portrayal of John and Jesus in the role of Elijah in Luke's birth stories and in the body of his Gospel remains.

John in the Body of Luke's Gospel

In the body of his Gospel Luke sometimes speaks favorably of John. He regularly uses the hyperbolic 'all' to describe the people's response to John's preaching. The people 'all were questioning in their hearts concerning John, whether he might be the Messiah' (Lk. 3.15; see also Lk. 3.3, 21; 7.29; Acts 13.24). Only Luke reports that Jesus' disciples asked him to teach them to pray as John taught his disciples (Lk. 11.1). Luke reports a saying of Jesus that extols John: 'Among those born of women no one is greater than John; yet the least in the kingdom of God is greater than he' (Lk. 7.28; Mt. 11.11). The fact that Luke regarded this saying as complimentary, not derogatory, is clear from his editorial addition:

> And all the people who heard this...acknowledged the justice of God, because they had been baptized with John's baptism. But by refusing to be baptized by him, the Pharisees and the lawyers rejected God's purpose for themselves (Lk. 7.29-30).

Luke retains the passage in which Jesus defends John, as well as himself, against his critics: 'John the Baptist has come eating no bread and drinking no wine, and you say, "He has a demon"' (Lk. 7.33; Mt. 11.18). As we have observed, this saying is one of the ways Luke ties the Gospel in with his story of John's infancy (see Lk. 1.15).

The first three Gospels agree that after living the life of a hermit John appears from the wilderness to preach a baptism of repentance. All three Gospels also have the statement by John that he is not worthy to untie the thong of the sandals of the one coming after him. And the same Gospels also report that John says that he baptizes with water but that the one coming after him will baptize with the Holy Spirit. Otherwise

4. Brown, *Birth*, pp. 275-79.

there are some significant differences in the accounts of the Baptist, especially in Luke.

As we have learned, Luke alone continues the quotation beyond Isa. 40.3 quoted in Mk 1.3 to precisely the point he wanted: 'all flesh shall see the salvation of God' (Lk. 3.6). This prophetic saying is probably best taken in light of what Luke says in his infancy narratives. There he makes sure the prophecy of universal salvation is applied to Jesus, not John. It is for 'all peoples' and 'a light for revelation to the Gentiles and glory to your people Israel' (Lk. 2.30-32; see also Lk. 2.11). The revelation to Simeon by the Holy Spirit about seeing the Lord's Messiah (Lk. 2.29-32) is being fulfilled in Jesus. And Lk. 3.5-6 has literarily and theologically tied the Gospel in with the infancy narrative.

We should keep these passages in mind when we remember that Horsley says Jesus came for the socioeconomic and political liberation of 'all the people'. For Luke salvation surely included religious liberation of the people from their sins, if that was not uppermost in his thought.

John and the Baptism of Jesus. With respect to the baptism of Jesus, in Mark Jesus is presented as one who comes, presumably as others came, and is baptized. There is not even a hint that John recognizes Jesus in any special way or as the one who is 'more powerful than' he (Mk 1.7; Mt. 3.11; Lk. 3.16). But in Matthew the situation is different. When Jesus comes to be baptized, John immediately recognizes him and says, 'I need to be baptized by you, and do you come to me?' But Jesus tells John to go ahead because it is proper to do so (Mt. 3.13-15). Remember that John was preaching 'a baptism of repentance for the forgiveness of sins' (Mk 1.4; Lk. 3.3). And Mark and Matthew both say that those baptized by John came 'confessing their sins' (Mk 1.6; Mt. 3.6). In *Pss. Sol.* 17.41 it is stated that the Messiah was to be 'pure from sin, in order to rule a great people'. Perhaps Matthew was influenced by a Jewish view similar to the one expressed in that psalm and therefore wrote that John consented to baptize Jesus, who Matthew believed was the Messiah.

In Luke's account of Jesus' baptism there are crucial differences between what Luke says compared with what Mark and Matthew say. Luke moves up the time of John's imprisonment to before the baptism of Jesus (Lk. 3.19-20). Both Mark and Matthew place the account of John's arrest later (Mk 6.17-18; Mt. 14.3-4). By stating that John was in prison Luke can logically omit any reference to John in speaking about the baptism of Jesus that follows immediately after the prison statement (Lk. 3.21-22). Luke simply says, 'Now when all the people were baptized, and when Jesus also had been baptized' (Lk. 3.21).

Among Luke's special interests is that of reporting that Jesus was a man of prayer (Lk. 5.16; 6.12; 9.18, 29; 11.1-4; 23.46). That interest becomes evident in his account of the baptism of Jesus. After Luke writes that Jesus was baptized, he continues by saying that when Jesus 'was praying, the heaven was opened, and the Holy Spirit descended upon him' (Lk. 3.21-22). By writing as he does, Luke avoids any hint that Jesus might be thought subordinate to John because Jesus was baptized by him. And, according to Luke, the Spirit came upon Jesus because he was praying, not because of his baptism by John. That is a unique Lukan touch.

In Acts Luke reflects differences, if not controversy, between followers of John and of Jesus. According to Acts 19.1-7, a group of people at Ephesus called 'disciples' had not received the Holy Spirit when they became believers. Why? Because they had been baptized with the baptism of John. John's baptism was thought ineffective because he did not baptize in the name of Jesus and did not practice the laying on of hands for the reception of the Holy Spirit. According to Luke in Acts, Paul described the baptism by John as one of repentance and asking people to believe in Jesus. Upon hearing Paul's words, 'they were baptized in the name of the Lord Jesus. When Paul had laid his hands on them, the Holy Spirit came upon them' (Acts 19.4-6). This passage indicates that the baptism practiced by John's followers was not condemned. It was just not adequate compared with that practiced by Jesus' apostles. Only baptism that provided a means for obtaining the Spirit was true baptism. After all, according to the Baptist himself, that was the kind of baptism Jesus was supposed to perform. The Baptist says, 'I baptize you with water; but the one who is more powerful than I...will baptize you with the Holy Spirit' (Lk. 3.16; see also Mk 1.8; Mt. 3.11). By saying that John baptized with water only, and not with the Spirit, Luke portrays John as inferior to Jesus.

John as a Prophet. After having observed Luke's portrayal of John as subordinate to Jesus or of Jesus as superior to John, let us look closely at Luke's account again. There are, as we have observed, times when Luke presents John in a favorable light. John will be called 'the prophet of the Most High' (Lk. 1.76) but Jesus 'the Son of the Most High' (Lk. 1.32). John is referred to as a prophet in spite of the fact that Luke has Jesus designated as prophet more often than any other Gospel writer (Lk. 7.16; 13.33; 24.19, passages only in Luke).

When Jewish authorities in Jerusalem questioned Jesus about his authority, Jesus asked them a question about John's authority that put them in a real dilemma. The Jews asked Jesus, 'By what authority are you doing these things? Who gave you this authority to do them?' Instead of answering, Jesus asked them a question, 'Did the baptism of John come from heaven, or was it of human origin?' That question put them in the dilemma, so the Jews answered, 'We do not know' because the crowd 'all regarded John as truly a prophet' (Mk 11.27-33).

Luke retains the reference in Mk 11.32 to John 'as truly a prophet' (Lk. 20.6). It is interesting, though, if not significant, that Luke omits Mark's 'truly', as does Matthew (21.26). Yet Lk. 20.6 does tie the Gospel in with the statement of John as a prophet in Lk. 1.76. One may suspect that the prediction that John would be a prophet who 'will go before the Lord to prepare his ways' (Lk. 1.76) was written under the influence of the Markan statement that the Baptist was coming to 'prepare the way of the Lord' (Mk 1.3; Mt. 3.3; Lk. 3.4).

Luke retains a saying of Jesus asking if his hearers went out to see John as 'a prophet'. Jesus replies, 'Yes, I tell you, and more than a prophet' (Lk. 7.26; Mt. 11.9). And Luke also retains a saying in which Jesus compliments or defends John against the accusation of having a demon (Lk. 7.33-34; Mt. 11.18-19).

After studying these passages in the body of Luke's Gospel, it seems certain that in the stories of John's infancy Luke is portraying John as truly something more than a prophet. If Luke found that portrayal in a pre-Lukan source, as the passages just cited from Mark and Matthew seem to indicate, then at least he let it stand.

Summary

It seems that the basic reason for Luke writing about John as he does in both the infancy narratives and the Gospel is christological. In the history of Israel John was the last great figure, but one more than an ordinary prophet. As that figure, he signaled the beginning of a new age and was himself the forerunner of the Messiah who was to initiate that new age. It was precisely that status which made John greater than others among those born of women (Lk. 7.28; Mt. 11.11). Yet, the person whose coming John was proclaiming was to be 'more powerful than' he (Lk. 3.16). He, Jesus, was the 'salvation...prepared in the presence of all peoples, a light for revelation to the Gentiles and for glory to your people Israel' (Lk. 2.30-32; see also Lk. 3.6).

Luke's christological convictions became, at the same time, a subtle polemic against those followers of the Baptist who had not accepted Jesus as the Messiah (see Lk. 3.15; 4.41) and had not joined the Christian movement. To what degree Luke was consciously writing an anti-Baptist polemic, or just using his sources, is hard to tell. However, I think that in view of his theological beliefs and literary style, Luke was primarily responsible for what he said. Perhaps he was not always consistent in what he wrote, but many authors, even including this one, sometimes have the same literary fallacy.

John and Jesus in the Gospel of John

The writer of the fourth Gospel specifically reports the Baptist as saying that he did not know Jesus until he saw the Spirit descending from heaven like a dove and remaining on him (Jn 1.25-34). John 1.25-34, though, is so loaded with the writer's own Christology that its historicity is highly suspect. Although the Baptist says that he did not know Jesus, the writer begins the passage by saying that when John saw Jesus coming toward him he exclaimed, 'Here is the Lamb of God who takes away the sin of the world!' (Jn 1.29). And the writer concludes the passage by placing his own Christology in the mouth of the Baptist: 'And I myself have seen and have testified that this [Jesus] is the Son of God' (Jn 1.34; see also Jn 1.18 and other passages).

The four Gospels present John as the forerunner of Jesus, his superior successor. As we have already observed, Lk. 3.4 ties the body of the Gospel in very well with the stories of John's infancy. All Gospels also report that John, as well as Jesus, had disciples and place those disciples in contrast to the disciples of Jesus (Mk 2.18; Mt. 9.14; Lk. 5.33; see also Mt. 11.2-6; Lk. 7.18-23; 11.1; Jn 1.35-42; 3.22-30; 4.1-2). The writer of the fourth Gospel goes further when he says that two of John's disciples left him to follow Jesus (Jn 1.35-42). This indicates that the two groups of disciples were in competition, if not in controversy, with each other. After John's death, an incident not reported by Luke, his disciples 'came and took his body, and laid it in a tomb' (Mk 6.29; Mt. 14.12).

Luke 3.15, a passage only in Luke, leaves no doubt that some Jews were at least questioning whether John was the Messiah: 'All were questioning in their hearts concerning John, whether he might be the Messiah'. Although the Jews only questioned 'in their hearts concerning John', Luke says that John 'answered all of them' as though they had actually asked him the question about messiahship audibly. John's reply, however, is not an answer to the question but a statement about his baptizing that evades the issue of messiahship. John baptizes with water, but one more powerful than he is coming and will baptize them with the Holy Spirit (Lk. 3.16).

In light of Luke's view of Jesus as superior to John and as the Messiah (Lk. 2.11, 26), it is surprising that in his Gospel Luke does not have John deny that he is the Messiah, as the writer of the fourth Gospel does (Jn 1.20; 3.28). But Luke does precisely that in Acts 13.23-25 (see below). How is the wasted opportunity in Lk. 3.15-16 to be explained? Perhaps Luke does implicitly what the writer of the fourth Gospel does explicitly, since the words about whether Jesus was the Messiah are those of Luke and are not put on the lips of the Baptist. The one more powerful and before whom the Baptist is unworthy is still to come.

By the time the Gospel of John was written, the question of messiahship was resolved. Its author felt compelled to have the Baptist emphatically deny that he was the Messiah: 'I am not the Messiah' (Jn 1.20; 3.28). The Baptist was, rather, 'the voice of one crying out in the wilderness' (Jn 1.23, from Isa. 40.3; see also Mk 1.3; Mt. 3.3; Lk. 3.4). Jesus, not John, is 'the Lamb of God who takes away the sin of the world! ... After me comes a man who ranks ahead of me, because he was before me' (Jn 1.29-30; see also Jn 1.36). The fourth Gospel also has the synoptic statement of the Baptist that he is not worthy to untie the thong of Jesus' sandals (Jn 1.27; Mk 1.7; Mt. 3.11; Lk. 3.16).

Several passages that follow the one about Jesus' sandals make it clear that the writer of the fourth Gospel is not only writing to subordinate the Baptist to Jesus, but is also writing to controvert the Baptist's followers. In contrast to the Baptist, who twice denies that he is the Messiah, Jesus is proclaimed as the Messiah by Andrew, one of John's disciples who left John to follow Jesus (Jn 1.41). According to the fourth Gospel, Jesus 'is making and baptizing more disciples than John' (Jn 4.1). And the Baptist is made to say of Jesus and himself: 'He must increase, but I must decrease' (Jn 3.30).

Luke and the author of the fourth Gospel share a number of ideas. One of them is the denial of the baptist that he is the expected Messiah. However, the Baptist's absolute statement of denial is not reported in the Gospel of Luke but in the book of Acts. There the Baptist's words are put in the mouth of Paul during a synagogue service in Antioch of Pisidia (Acts 13.23-25):

> God has brought to Israel a Savior, Jesus, as he promised; before his coming John had already proclaimed a baptism of repentance to all the people of Israel. And as John was finishing his work, he said, 'What do you suppose that I am? I am not he. No, but one is coming after me; I am not worthy to untie the thong of the sandals on his feet.'

With these statements from Acts about John, including the reported statement of John himself, recall and compare what we observed about John and Jesus in God's plan for the salvation of humankind, according to Luke. The statements further confirm what we have observed with respect to that idea in Luke's Gospel.

Acts 18.24–19.7 reflects strong differences, if not controversy, between followers of John and of Jesus. Thus, it seems clear that by the time the Gospel of John and the book of Acts were written the followers of the Baptist and those of Jesus were rival groups.

The Baptist's existence is attested by Josephus, who writes that he was very popular among the Jews. Josephus says that the defeat of the army of Herod Antipas, son of Herod the Great, was divine vengeance for his treatment of John, who was surnamed the Baptist:

> He was a good man and commanded the Jews to cultivate virtue, to practice justice towards one another and piety toward God, and so doing to join in baptism... When others joined the crowds about him, because they were aroused to the highest degree upon hearing his words, Herod became alarmed, lest eloquence of so great an effect on mankind might lead to some form of sedition, for it looked as if they would be guided by John in everything they did (*Ant.* 18.5.2).[5]

Josephus goes on to say that Antipas decided to strike first before John's work led to some revolt and therefore had him put to death. From what Josephus says we can understand why some Jews might have regarded John as the Messiah. But Luke and the author of the fourth Gospel did not want that view to prevail.

5. Although the authenticity of this passage has been disputed by some scholars, I think most regard it as authentic.

Chapter 8

LUKE'S STORIES OF THE SHEPHERDS AND OF JESUS AND HIS PARENTS

Story of the Shepherds

The birth of Jesus during the reign of Augustus (27 BCE–14 CE) is probably a fact of history (Lk. 2.1). But Luke's story of the shepherds with the multitude (Greek, 'army') of angels is certainly a myth. We have already observed that of the Gospel writers only Luke has a special interest in the appearance of angels, not only in the birth stories but also in the rest of his Gospel and in Acts.

As a unit, Lk. 2.8-20 could be removed from Luke's narratives without disrupting the story. Luke 2.21 follows naturally after Lk. 2.7 and forms a conclusion to Lk. 2.1-7. At the same time, Lk. 2.20 is an appropriate conclusion to a unit that begins with Lk. 2.8. We may suspect, therefore, that Luke composed the story of the shepherds and angels and inserted it into the story of Jesus' birth between Lk. 2.7 and 2.21. Luke 2.21, then, serves as a conclusion to the whole larger unit, Lk. 2.1-21.

In Lk. 2.17-18 we read that after the shepherds saw the baby Jesus 'they made known what had been told them about this child; and all who heard it were amazed at what the shepherds told them'. These verses are a connecting link with the Gospel in Lk. 4.15, 'He began to teach in their synagogues and was praised by everyone'.

If Jesus was born in December (the popular view) it was not unlikely that even then shepherds would have been 'living in the fields, keeping watch over their flock by night'. Although during December rains may be heavy in Palestine, shepherds probably would be living outdoors and grazing their sheep, since grass grows in much of Palestine during winter.

Luke's phrase *en tē chōra* (Lk. 2.8) here means 'in the field' (as in Jn 4.35), as is clear from his word *agrauleō* (compare *agros*, 'field'), which means 'spend the night in the open' or 'bivouac'. Perhaps it also means to 'live in the fields'. It occurs in the New Testament only in Lk. 2.8, does not occur in the Septuagint and is rare elsewhere. That makes it hard for us to decide exactly what the word *agrauleō* does mean. So who knows where Luke got the word. The use of the word is just one instance that helps to support the view that Luke composed the shepherd story himself.

Although there are a number of words in the birth stories that Luke uses elsewhere in his Gospel, 'shepherd' is not one of them. He uses the word only in Lk. 2.8-20. But that is not the whole picture. Both Matthew and Luke retain two passages from Mark (6.34; 14.27) in which the word shepherd is used. Matthew (14.14) omits the word in the first passage, but he had used Mark's phrase, 'like sheep without a shepherd', in Mt. 9.36. Matthew retains Mark's phrase 'I will strike the shepherd' from Mk 14.27 in Mt. 26.31. Moreover, he also uses the word shepherd in Mt. 25.32, a passage only in Matthew's Gospel. Luke, on the other hand, omits the word shepherd from both Mk 6.34 and 14.27 in Lk. 9.11 and 22.39-40.

It seems clear that Luke intentionally avoided the use of the word shepherd in the body of his Gospel. It seems strange, then, does it not, that he has the story of the shepherds and angels in the stories of Jesus' birth? If he found the pericope already circulating in earlier Christian tradition, he must have used it for some special purpose, because he avoided the word shepherd elsewhere in his Gospel. But what about shepherds themselves? What kinds of fellows were they?

What Kinds of Persons Were Shepherds?

Many people today may think of shepherds as gentle, nonaggressive, even affectionate persons. Those who think that way probably have been influenced by some passages in the Bible, especially Psalm 23—'The Lord is my shepherd'. And there is also that well-known metaphor of Jesus as the good shepherd, who was even willing to lay down his life for his sheep (Jn 10.11-18).

There were undoubtedly some good shepherds. However, it seems that shepherds in general had bad reputations. We can detect this feeling toward them in the story of Jesus as the good shepherd in the Gospel of John. Indeed, the words put on the lips of Jesus by the author—'I am the *good* shepherd' (my emphasis)—imply that there were bad shepherds. This is made clear by the author when he had Jesus say earlier, 'I am the gate [one of the author's metaphors] for the sheep. All who came before me are thieves and bandits; but the sheep did not listen to them' (Jn 10.7-8, 11, 14). In contrast to those kinds of shepherds, Jesus was the good shepherd.

In the era of the rabbis shepherds were frequently regarded as dishonest, as robbers, and as other lawless persons, because they often grazed their herds on lands belonging to someone else. One rabbi said, 'You will find that there is no more contemptible occupation in the world than that of shepherds'.[1] Such evidence has been used by Goulder and others to show 'Luke's predilection...for the salvation of the shady'. On the other hand, Brown does not think that we can use the sayings of the rabbis as evidence for shepherds as dubious characters in the time of Luke.[2] Nor does Fitzmyer.[3]

There is other evidence, though, that has to be considered when we think of shepherds in the time of Luke. From the beginning of Hebrew history there was antagonism between farmers and shepherds. The Old Testament story about the brothers Cain and Abel (Gen. 4.1-16) already reflects that antagonism, and it ended in the ultimate tragedy for one of the characters. Abel, 'a keeper of sheep', was murdered by his jealous brother Cain, 'a tiller of the ground'. The tragedy clearly reflects the conflict between shepherding and farming as ways of life among the Hebrew people.

A Greek inscription, dating from 221 BCE reads: 'Command Diophanes...not to overlook me who am being maltreated in a lawless way by the shepherds'.[4] At least one inscription, of which I am aware, comes from the time of Jesus. It is dated 42 CE and reads: 'The shepherds let their flocks into the pasturage which I have in the olive-yard of Thermoutharion'.[5] Those shepherds apparently grazed their sheep on the pasturelands of others.

If Luke was aware of shepherds being regarded as such rascally fellows, his awareness might explain why he omitted any reference to shepherds in the body of his Gospel. But such awareness would make

1. For this and other sayings of the same kind see Goulder, *Luke*, I, pp. 251-52.
2. Brown, *Birth*, pp. 625-26, 673.
3. Fitzmyer, *Gospel*, I, p. 396.
4. From James H. Moulton and George Milligan, *The Vocabulary of the Greek Testament* (London: Hodder & Stoughton, 1949), p. 524.
5. Moulton and Milligan, *Vocabulary*, p. 524.

his use of them in the birth narratives all the more curious. He must have used them, then, to serve a particular purpose, about which I will speak in a moment. But first let me point out a prominent aspect of Luke's writing style in the story of the shepherds.

Luke's Literary Style in the Story of the Shepherds

The story of the shepherds contains several aspects of Luke's peculiar literary style. Besides his special interest in angels, here is just one more example. In the line where Luke first mentions shepherds the clause translated as 'keeping watch over their flock by night' is literally, 'watching the watches of the night over their flock' (Lk. 2.8). Phrases such as 'watching the watches' are known as cognate expressions, whereby a verb ('to watch') is followed by its noun ('watches'). In Greek Luke's phrase is *phylassontes phylakas*.

Luke uses a similar expression again in the next verse (Lk. 2.9): 'They were terrified' is in Greek, 'They were afraid with a great fear' or 'they feared a great fear' (*ephobēthēsan phobon megan*). Such cognate expressions are characteristic of Luke's literary style elsewhere, for example: 'baptized with the baptism of John' (Lk. 7.29); 'you load persons with loads' (Lk. 11.46); and 'I have desired with a desire' (Lk. 22.15). In light of Luke's literary style so obvious in the narrative of the shepherds, let me now suggest why he probably composed that narrative.

Purpose of the Story of the Shepherds

Some scholars—Goulder among them, as we have learned—have suggested that the shepherds symbolize sinners whom Jesus came to save. This view is supported with the angel's statement to the shepherds: 'To you is born this day in the city of David a Savior, who is the Messiah, the Lord' (Lk. 2.11). It ties the birth narratives in well with statements of Luke in the body of the Gospel. See, for example, 'I have come to call not the righteous but sinners to repentance' (Lk. 5.32; see also Lk. 4.43; 15.1-7). The inscriptions quoted above would, of course, support the view that the shepherds represented sinners and were among those whom Luke thought Jesus came to save.

Other scholars have proposed that Luke was influenced by Greek mystery (secret) religions. In the mythology of Mithraism it is told that shepherds came respectfully to present gifts in the form of firstfruits from their crops and herds to the infant god Mithras. Still other scholars think the shepherds represent either the economically poor or the spiritually depressed.[6]

Fitzmyer is firm in saying that, in spite of rabbinic tradition, shepherds do not represent sinners to whom salvation was announced by the angels. Nor, according to Fitzmyer, are they examples of the poor, because 'their flock' may mean that they owned the animals. Their appearance 'is another example in the infancy narrative of Luke's predilection for the lowly of human society' (see Lk. 1.52).[7] But how lowly would the shepherds be regarded if they weren't poor? In fact, a basic element in the word translated as 'lowly' (*tapeinos*) in Lk. 1.52 is 'poor', in the sense 'of low estate'. That is one of the reasons why shepherds were despised. Luke uses the word only in 1.58, and it appears only a few times elsewhere in the New Testament. In Jas 1.9-10 it is used in contrast to the rich (*plousios*).

Horsley emphatically disagrees with Fitzmyer that Luke's interest is in the lowly. Nor, according to Horsley, were 'shepherds a specially despised group of people in first-century Palestine'. However, 'their status in the society generally was probably very low'. Horsley quotes Philo (*Agr.* 14) to support his viewpoint: 'Such pursuits [as the herding of sheep and goats] are held mean and inglorious...most of all in the eyes of kings'. According to Horsley, two points belong together in Luke's story: 'the messiah and savior has been born in the midst of and indeed as one of the ordinary people, and the shepherds as the obvious local representative of those ordinary people are called to witness and proclaim the good news of the eventual liberation the child represents'.[8] Aha! 'Herod is Herod', according to Horsley, and does not represent anything. But the shepherds do! They are 'obvious local representatives of those ordinary people...'

Now let's think a bit about what we have observed. How much difference should we attribute to the designations 'lowly' and 'ordinary people' in the time of Jesus? If one takes 'lowly' in the sense of 'relating to a low social or economic rank', as Horsley does, how many of the ordinary people belonged to a higher rank? Moreover, if we read elsewhere in Philo (*Agr.* 9), Horsley's support for what he says about shepherds is considerably weakened. Philo writes:

6. See Horsley, *Liberation*, p. 106.
7. Fitzmyer, *Gospel*, I, p. 396.
8. Horsley, *Liberation*, pp. 100, 103, 104.

> Shepherds have to show much forethought that their flocks do not come down with disease because of negligence and laziness, even praying that plagues against which there is no protection do not strike the sheep... So, at least, the job of being a shepherd has been thought to be so august and profitable that poets are accustomed to giving kings the title of 'shepherds of the people' (*Agr.* 9-10).

Although this passage may contradict what I said about shepherds as being rascals, it also contradicts the view that their status in society was very low.

The Messiah was to be descended from David, the hero of God and of his fellow Israelites, a shepherd boy who bragged about killing lions and bears while tending his father's sheep (1 Sam. 16.11-13; 17.12-51). Since David's home had been in Bethlehem, some scholars think that Luke used the story of the shepherds to support the tradition of Jesus' birth in that city.[9]

Frankly, we do not know why Luke uses the shepherd story in the account of Jesus' birth, especially since he avoids mentioning shepherds in the body of his Gospel. In view of Luke's special interest in the poor and lowly, it is strange that he did not put shepherds in the body of his Gospel, especially since they were in his sources. Anyhow, I think the following observations are helpful in trying to understand why Luke used the shepherd pericope, if he did not actually compose it, as I believe he did.

Luke tells us that Jesus was born in the time of Emperor Augustus, and only Luke mentions Augustus. As the founder of the Roman Empire, Augustus brought peace to the world by putting an end to the devastating wars after Julius Caesar was murdered. The age of Augustus became known as the *pax Romana*, 'the peace of Rome'. It brought with it not only the end of war but also order within the Empire. For thousands of Romans the *pax Romana* meant the fulfillment of 'the glorious age' that the poet Virgil had predicted (*Eclogue* 4.11).

From ancient inscriptions we learn that, among other Roman emperors, Augustus was hailed as 'savior of the world'. Compare Jn 4.42, where it is said of Jesus: 'This is truly the Savior of the world' (see also 1 Jn 4.14). Luke could, therefore, easily have intentionally written that Augustus issued a decree that affected the whole Roman world. An inscription referring to Augustus, who was regarded as a god as well as

9. For other proposals as to why Luke included the incident of the shepherds and angels in his birth narratives see Brown, *Birth*, pp. 392-34, 672-75.

savior, reads: 'The birthday of the god was for the world the beginning of tidings [Greek, *euangelion*] of joy on his account'.[10]

It is true, as Horsley says, that the *pax Romana* was imposed by military might, but that it 'meant subjection' goes too far with respect to the Jews. Even if one thinks of subjection as a relative term, Horsley ignores all the passages in Josephus that describe the *freedoms* given the Jews by Augustus.[11]

Within Luke's story of the shepherds there are at least three phenomena associated with Augustus that Luke mentions. First, joy at the birth of Jesus: 'I am bringing you good news [Greek, *euangelizomi*] of great joy for all the people' (Lk. 2.10). Second, reference to Jesus as Savior: 'a Savior, who is the Messiah, the Lord' (Lk. 2.11). And third, peace, as the result of Jesus' coming: 'on earth peace among those whom he [God] favors' (Lk. 2.14).

It seems to me that the evidence just does not support the idea that 'Luke clearly understands Jesus to be in direct confrontation with the emperor'.[12] How did Luke think Jesus would confront the emperor, with military might? I think the point is not confrontation but contrast between Jesus and Augustus.

In a subtle way Luke was writing politico-evangelism directed toward both Jews and Gentiles. The birth of Jesus, not that of Augustus, was the real reason for 'good news of great joy for all the people' (Lk. 2.10). And 'a multitude of the heavenly host', not human beings, proclaimed the birth of Jesus. Yet, all human beings whom the Most High God, not the god Augustus, favored were to experience the peace Jesus came to bring.

Peace is a favorite theme of Luke, not only in the stories of Jesus' birth but also in the rest of the Gospel. 'Peace' occurs five times in Luke only in the body of his Gospel (Lk. 7.50; 14.32; 19.38, 42; 24.36; see also Lk. 8.48; 10.5-6; 12.51). Although sometimes for Luke 'peace' means the absence of war (Lk. 11.21; 14.32; 19.42), more often it is used in the sense of a human state of existence that Jesus came to bring.

10. From Adolf Deissmann, *Light from the Ancient East* (trans. L.R.M. Strachan; New York: Doran, 1927), p. 366.

11. Horsley, *Liberation*, p. 28. For Augustus and the Jews see Emil Schürer, *The History of the Jewish People in the Age of Jesus Christ*, III.1 (rev. and ed. G. Vermes, F. Millar and M. Goodman; Edinburgh: T. & T. Clark, 1986), pp. 116-21.

12. Horsley, *Liberation*, p. 33.

In the birth stories Zechariah speaks of guiding 'our feet into the way of peace' (Lk. 1.79). It is the kind of peace about which Simeon speaks, 'Now you are dismissing your servant in peace' (Lk. 2.29), and the peace of which the angels sing (Lk. 2.14), 'peace among people of good will' (my trans.). Fitzmyer gives reasons why *en anthrōpois eudokias* should be translated as 'for people whom he [God] favors' (Brown, 'to those favored [by Him]').[13] But in this case I think the choice is arbitrary. Regardless of the translation, 'peace' surely includes more than the absence of military conflict for the people Luke had in mind.

Jesus instructed his disciples to tell people as they went along, 'Peace to this house' (Lk. 10.5). Perhaps the most important passage for our purposes is Luke's account of Jesus' entry into Jerusalem. Although the three synoptic writers report that incident in Jesus' life, only Luke has a statement about peace. Just as the multitude of angels proclaimed peace and glory to the shepherds at the birth of Jesus (Lk. 2.13-14), so did 'the whole multitude of the disciples' when Jesus entered Jerusalem: 'Peace in heaven, and glory in the highest heaven' (Lk. 19.37-38). Here peace and glory are both heavenly qualities.[14] According to Acts 10.36, God sent a message 'to the people of Israel, preaching peace by Jesus Christ' (see also Acts 9.31).

According to Luke, Jesus was not only a Savior; he was also 'Messiah Lord' (*christos kyrios*; Lk. 2.11). The expression 'Messiah Lord' occurs nowhere else in the same way in the New Testament (see 'the Lord's Messiah' in Lk. 2.26). According to Luke in Acts 2.36, God made Jesus 'both Lord and Messiah' (see 'Lord Messiah' in the *Psalms of Solomon*). Luke not only portrays Jesus as superior to John, a Jew, but he also uses the story of the shepherds as a foil for portraying the superiority of Jesus to the great Augustus, a Gentile.

Augustus brought a new age in Roman history, but Jesus came to bring a new era in world history, both religiously and socially. But what the political-economic overtones of Luke's Jesus as Messiah and Lord and as a peace-bringer are is still an open question. It seems to me, though, that there is little evidence for thinking Luke meant to portray Jesus as a political revolutionary.

The shepherds went to Bethlehem 'to see this thing that has taken place, which the Lord has made known to us' (Lk. 2.15). Then they spread 'the good news of great joy for all the people' about the 'Savior,

13. Fitzmyer, *Gospel*, I, pp. 411-12; Brown, *Birth*, pp. 393, 403-405.

14. See Fitzmyer, *Gospel*, I, p. 1251.

who is the Messiah, the Lord... They made known what had been told them about this child; and all who heard it were amazed at what the shepherds told them' (Lk. 2.15-18). All this was written with the hope of winning converts to the Christian movement, including not only followers of John the Baptist but also admirers, even devotees, of Augustus.

The Last Two Pericopes in Luke's Birth Narratives

The last two pericopes in Luke's stories of Jesus' birth are the presentation of Jesus in the temple (Lk. 2.22-40) and Jesus' experience in the temple as a boy of 12 years old (Lk. 2.41-52). The stories are independent units of material, each with separate beginnings (Lk. 2.22 and 2.41) and endings (Lk. 2.39-40 and 2.51-52). In each pericope Joseph and Mary are referred to as the parents of Jesus (Lk. 2.27, 41, 43). In each pericope Joseph is called the father of Jesus (Lk. 2.33, 48). And in each pericope the temple in Jerusalem is the scene of the action. These are the unifying bonds in the two narratives.

'Parents' (*goneis*) is a favorite word of Luke's. Twice (Lk. 8.56; 18.29) he inserts the word where it does not occur in his source Mark (Mk 5.43; 10.29 = Mt. 19.29). And the one time Mark uses the word, Luke retains it (Lk. 21.16; Mk 13.12 = Mt. 10.21).

Besides 'parents', other words characteristic of Luke are the verb *poreuomai*, meaning to 'travel', 'journey' or 'go' (Mark, 3 times; Matthew, 29 times; Luke, 51 in the Gospel and 38 in Acts). It is translated as 'went' in Lk. 2.41. The words *kata to ethos* (three times in Luke, but nowhere else in the New Testament), translated 'as usual' (lit. 'according to custom') in the NRSV of Lk. 2.42, are only Lukan. Another characteristic Lukan expression is the word *odynaomai*, meaning 'feel acute pain', physical or mental, which occurs three times in Luke, once in Acts, but nowhere else in the New Testament. It is translated as 'in great anxiety' in Lk. 2.48. By using these words Luke certainly adapts the two pericopes to his own style and ties them in with the content elsewhere in the Gospel. Other Lukan traits in the two pericopes under consideration are a revelation of the Holy Spirit to Simeon, who was then guided by the Spirit (Lk. 2.25-27), the two summaries in Lk. 2.40 and 2.52, and Jerusalem as a place of special interest (see below).

Although we cannot be certain about the original source and content of the two pericopes, they must have come from a time and place before the tradition of a virginal conception of Jesus arose. Or, at least, the tradition was not yet widely known. If Luke did not compose the stories, he certainly Lukanized them with his own vocabulary and literary style. I am inclined to think that Luke composed the pericopes himself.

Presentation of Jesus in the Temple

It is generally agreed that Matthew is certainly one of the most Jewish authors among New Testament writers and that he has a special interest in the Jewish law. On the other hand, it is also generally agreed that Luke is one of the most Gentile writers and that, theoretically at least, he should not have a special interest in Jewish law. One would expect, therefore, to find the stories of the presentation of a firstborn son and the purification of the mother after childbirth according to Old Testament law in Matthew's infancy story, not in Luke's.

It is clear, though, that Luke is not very familiar with the law of Moses to which he alludes. 'Their purification' (Lk. 2.22) means that both parents had to be purified, but the law in Leviticus 12 makes no reference to the father. According to that law, a woman who gave birth to a male child was considered ritually unclean for 7 days before the circumcision of the boy and for 33 days after that. During those 40 days the woman was not to touch any holy thing or go into the sanctuary. The law was twice as stringent for a woman who gave birth to a female baby: 'If she bears a female child, she shall be unclean two weeks' and 'her time of blood purification shall be sixty-six days' (Lev. 12.2-5).

According to Hebrew law, after her purification, a woman who had given birth to either a son or a daughter was to take 'a lamb in its first year for a burnt offering, and a pigeon or a turtledove for a sin offering' to the temple. The priest would then make the offering to the Lord (Lev. 12.6-7). If the woman could not afford a sheep, she was to take 'two turtledoves or two pigeons', one for a burnt offering and the other for a sin offering (Lev. 12.8). Since Luke says that Mary and Joseph took the birds and not the lamb, does he mean to indicate that they were too poor to afford a lamb? This is the usual view.

Perhaps the doves were symbolic of the Spirit, as at Jesus' baptism, where the Holy Spirit descends on Jesus 'like a dove' (Mk 1.10; Mt. 3.16; Lk. 3.22; Jn 1.32). After the sacrifice of the doves, 'the Holy Spirit rested on' Simeon, who previously experienced a revelation by the Holy Spirit (Lk. 2.25-26).

There are several more perplexing questions, it seems to me, than those raised about Luke and Hebrew law concerning purification after childbirth. Among the ancient Hebrews, the birth of a child was thought to be defiling, therefore purification was necessary afterward. That is why one of the offerings was to be a 'sin offering'. Of course, most people in our society no longer regard childbirth as defiling, so that raises a theological question for us, does it not?

We have learned that while still a virgin Mary became pregnant by the action of the Holy Spirit with God's favor announced by the angel Gabriel sent by God. Why, then, would Mary have to make a sin offering after the process of giving birth as with an ordinary Jewish woman? Would God really expect that of Mary if he had told her that she would become pregnant and bear a child, an extraordinary child at that? Would not the miracle of Jesus' birth make the purification of Mary unnecessary? Think about it.

The clause 'every firstborn male shall be designated as holy to the Lord' (Lk. 2.23) is an allusion to Exod. 13.2, 11-15, where the Lord requests that the firstborn of human beings and animals is to be consecrated to him. Originally such firstborn humans were to serve God in some special way for the rest of their lives. Eventually, however, the Levites (temple officials) were selected to perform the services of the cult, so the firstborn were relieved of that responsibility (Num. 8.14-19). Here, as often elsewhere, the story of Elkanah and Hannah and their young son Samuel was the model for much of what Luke writes.

Jesus in the Temple at the Age of Twelve

Among the first three Gospel writers, only Luke is interested in even a partial chronology of Jesus' life. He mentions the baby's circumcision 'after eight days had passed', again in conformity with Jewish law (Lk. 2.21). Then we know nothing of Jesus' life until his parents, as faithful observant Jews, took him along with them to the temple in Jerusalem for the festival of Passover when he was 12 years of age (Lk. 2.41-42). And, finally, Luke writes: 'Jesus was about thirty years old when he began his work' (Lk. 3.23; see also Jn 8.57).

Because the last pericope in Luke's stories (Lk. 2.41-52) is somewhat different from the preceding one in literary style and effect, it may reflect a later stage in composition. The behavior of young Jesus in the temple resembles the stories of so-called 'hidden years', an expression often used to designate the time Jesus spent at home before he began his public life. The years are 'hidden' because the Gospels in the New Testament report nothing about Jesus during that time. However, those years became a biographical concern of the authors of certain apocryphal gospels from the second century.

Stories of Precocious Youths. There are interesting, though apocryphal, stories of Jesus' exceptional boyhood in the *Infancy Gospel of Thomas*. For example, at 5 years of age Jesus made 12 sparrows from soft clay on the sabbath. Because Jesus had made the birds on the Sabbath, a Jew who saw what he did was disturbed. Why? Because making the birds was considered work, and that meant disobeying the commandment forbidding work on the sabbath day (Exod. 20.8-11; Deut. 5.12-15). When Joseph, Jesus' father, was told about Jesus thus profaning the Sabbath, and when his father scolded him for his behavior, 'Jesus clapped his hands and cried to the sparrows: "Off with you!" And the sparrows took flight and went away chirping. The Jews were amazed when they saw this, and went away and told their elders what they had seen Jesus do' (*Thomas* 2.1-5).

Below is another interesting story of the same kind from the same gospel.

> When he [Jesus] was six years old, his mother gave him a pitcher and sent him to draw water and bring it into the house. But in the crowd he stumbled, and the pitcher was broken. But Jesus spread out the garment he was wearing, filled it with water and brought it to his mother. And when his mother saw the miracle, she kissed him, and kept within herself the mysteries which she had seen him do (*Thomas* 11.1).

With the last sentence in the quotation compare these statements in Luke: 'Mary treasured all these words and pondered them in her heart' (Lk. 2.19) and 'His mother treasured all these things in her heart' (Lk. 2.51). In the first quotation the phrase 'all these words' refers to what the shepherds had heard about Jesus from the angels. In the second quotation 'all these things' refer to what Jesus had done in the temple and what he had told his parents about being in his Father's house.

There is also the apocryphal story about a Jewish teacher by the name of Zacchaeus who asked Jesus' father for permission to teach his son. But when he began to teach Jesus, the boy so greatly confounded the teacher that he asked Joseph to take him away. After exclaiming about the greatness of the boy, Zacchaeus finally says, 'He is something great, a god or an angel or what I should say I do not know' (*Thomas* 7.4).[15]

15. These stories are taken from E. Hennecke, *New Testament Apocrypha*

According to Luke, when in the temple at 12 years of age, Jesus was 'sitting among the teachers, listening to them and asking them questions. And all who heard him were amazed at his understanding and his answers' (Lk. 2.46-47).

There are other stories in the *Infancy Gospel of Thomas* like the ones quoted. Although Luke's story of Jesus in the temple at 12 is much less fanciful and more refined than the stories quoted, it was also intended to show the uniqueness of the boy Jesus.

Stories of precocious youths whose ages range from 10 to 14 years abound in literature of the ancient world. Below are examples from several different sources.

In his autobiography Josephus boasts about his own academic acumen as a young man:

> While still a mere boy, about fourteen years old, I was commended by everyone because of my love of letters, so that the high priests and leading men of the city always came to me in order to learn about some precise point concerning our customs (*Life*, 2).

Insofar as I know, there is no evidence in other sources that confirms Josephus's boast. There are no honor rolls or official school reports available from Josephus's time.

Josephus retells many Old Testament narratives with interesting embellishments. In writing about Moses he says that Moses was the noblest Hebrew of all with respect to intelligence and accomplishments. When he was three years old, God gave Moses 'an amazing increase of stature'. But 'his understanding [*synesis*] was not in accordance with his stature [*hēlikia*], but was far superior to the number of his years' (*Ant*. 2.9.6). The first word within parentheses is the same word that Luke uses with reference to Jesus in Lk. 2.47: 'All who heard him were amazed at his understanding [*synesis*] and his answers'. The second word occurs in Lk. 2.52: 'And Jesus increased in wisdom and in stature [*hēlikia*]'.

What Josephus says about Samuel is even more interesting and relevant to our discussion: 'Having completed his twelfth year, Samuel was already holding the office of prophet' (*Ant*. 5.10.4). Although the Old Testament account portrays Samuel as an exceptional youth, there is nothing said about him being 12 years of age. We have observed that

(2 vols.; ed. W. Schneemelcher; trans. R. McL. Wilson; London: Lutterworth, 1963–1964), I, pp. 393, 395, 396.

the story of Samuel was a model for Luke's birth stories. Is it probable that when Luke wrote about Jesus at 12 he was familiar with the tradition preserved by Josephus with respect to Samuel's age? Or did Luke and Josephus each use a common Jewish source containing legends about Samuel?

Philo speaks of Moses as advanced beyond his age in intellectual capacity, surpassing that of teachers from different parts of the world. Moses actually devised problems that those teachers found it difficult to solve (*Vit. Mos.* 1.5). Recall the apocryphal story about the Jewish teacher who was confounded by Jesus.

Perhaps the closest parallel to Luke's story of Jesus at 12 years of age is that of the Hellenistic writer Plutarch, whom I cited in Chapter 3 in connection with the Holy Spirit coming upon Mary so that she conceived Jesus. In writing about the life of Alexander the Great Plutarch mentions his outstanding abilities while still a boy. Alexander

> once entertained the envoys from the Persian king who came during Philip's [Alexander's father] absence, and associated with them fully. He won...them by his friendliness, and by asking no childish or trivial questions... The envoys were therefore astonished and regarded the much-talked-of ability of Philip as nothing compared with his son's eager disposition to do great things.[16]

Suetonius writes about Augustus: 'In his twelfth year he delivered a funeral oration to the assembled people in honour of his grandmother... He received offices and honours before the usual age, and some of a new kind and for life.'[17]

Perhaps in the stories of the conception of Jesus and of Jesus at 12 in the temple Luke shows influence from the Hellenism of his time, represented by the authors quoted. The Hellenistic writers emphasize the intelligence of the boys. Jesus' keen mind is the central element in Luke's story of Jesus in the temple at 12 as well.

According to Plutarch, the young Alexander, as with Jesus, asked the authorities questions. In the account of Luke, as in that of Plutarch, the parents were not present when the boys were in the company of their, supposedly, superiors and questioning them. And in both accounts those who heard the boys were amazed.

16. Plutarch, *Lives*, 'Alexander' 4; trans. from LCL, VII, p. 235.
17. Suetonius, *Lives*, 'Augustus' 8, 26; trans. from LCL, I, pp. 131, 159.

Before leaving Luke's story of Jesus in the temple at 12 years of age we should observe several other things. As a typical part of his literary style, Luke twice summarizes Jesus' maturing growth (Lk. 2.40, 52). The first summary comes at the end of the pericope dealing with the purification of Jesus' parents, the second, at the end of the temple story. In this emphatic way, as we have observed, Luke ties the stories of Jesus' birth in with the body of the Gospel: 'All spoke well of him and were amazed at the gracious words that came from his mouth' (Lk. 4.22).

With Lk. 2.40, 52 and 4.22 compare Lk. 11.49, where Luke alone uses the words 'the Wisdom of God said' to introduce a saying from an unidentifiable source. We cannot be certain whether 'the Wisdom of God' is meant to refer to God or to Jesus. The summaries in the birth narratives may indicate that Luke wanted his readers to understand Jesus himself. Jesus' hometown folks asked, 'What is this wisdom that has been given to him?' (Mk 6.2; see also Mt. 13.54). And several passages from Paul's letters support the view of Jesus as the Wisdom of God. See, for example, 1 Cor. 1.24, 'Christ the power of God and the wisdom of God' and 'Christ Jesus, who became for us wisdom from God' (1 Cor. 1.30; see also 1 Cor. 2.7; Col. 2.2-3). The tradition that wisdom was a special feature of the superior nature of Jesus is strong.

Jesus and his Parents

In the pericope of Jesus in the temple as a boy (Lk. 2.41-51) Luke mentions Jesus' 'father and mother'. Luke also refers to Joseph and Mary as 'his parents'. Notice especially that when Joseph and Mary find Jesus, Mary scolds him a little: 'Child, why have you treated us like this? Look, your father and I have been searching for you in great anxiety.' Mary should know better than anyone else who the father of Jesus really was, should she not? Indeed, she does know because she says plainly, '*your father* and I'.

From what the angel told Mary she really knew that her son was to be very different from other children. And if he was so precocious that he amazed all who observed 'his understanding and his answers', why were she and Joseph concerned to the point of 'great anxiety' when he was lost (Lk. 2.47-48)? The question has even more weight if Mary knew that Jesus was 'the Son of the Most High' and had all the other great qualities that had been told her by the angel, does it not? Jesus' parents did not even understand what he meant about being in his

Father's house. But, as is typical, perhaps, the loving mother, Mary, 'treasured all these things in her heart' (Lk. 2.51). Apparently it was the things she recently realized about Jesus that Mary treasured. Notice that Jesus, like every good Jewish boy, continued to obey his parents: 'was obedient to them' (Lk. 2.51).

On the other hand, could it be that Mary was so concerned about Jesus because she was aware of his precocial nature? But if that is true, then wouldn't she lack faith in what the angel had told her? At any rate, if we had only the passage in Lk. 2.41-51, there would be no question about who the father of Jesus was, would there?

Most Christians, including commentators, rarely speak of Joseph as though he was the natural father of Jesus, obviously for theological reasons. I have already spoken about betrothal, marriage and divorce in Jewish society. Now I consider briefly the concept of 'father' and adoption.

Goulder says that ' "father" was the normal word for adoptive father in a much-bereaved society'. As evidence for adoption as a common phenomenon in the ancient world he refers to Jn 19.26 and Acts 7.21.[18] At the outset, I should say that if Joseph was the adoptive father of Jesus such adoption would have fanned the flames of suspicion of the illegitimacy of Jesus in the minds of his Jewish critics who were making the accusation.

With respect to Jn 19.26, 'the disciple took [*elaben*] her [Mary] into his own home', the verb *lambanō* means no more than what it says: 'take' or 'accept'. Did the beloved disciple do more than consent to take care of Mary? We have seen that Joseph 'took (*parelaben*) his wife (Mt. 1.25), but it is not said that Joseph 'took' Jesus. Joseph's acceptance of Jesus was in giving him a name, which, after all, the angel had told him to do.

In Acts 7.21, in Stephen's speech, composed by Luke, of course, it is said that Pharaoh's daughter adopted Moses. The word translated as 'adopted' really means 'lifted up' (*aneilatō*), and Stephen's words are based on LXX Exod. 2.5-10. However, in common Greek the verb *anaireō* had come to mean 'adopt' in the sense of officially acknowledging a baby as one's own. We know this from ancient inscriptions and other sources. But that word is not used with reference to Joseph and the baby Jesus.

18. Goulder, *Luke*, I, pp. 262, 267.

In both the Hebrew and Greek texts of Exod. 2.10 it says that when the child was grown Moses' mother took him to Pharaoh's daughter. And both texts say, 'He became to her for a son' (NRSV, 'she took him as her son'). The words of the original texts, 'He became to her for a son', may reflect an adoption formula. If they do mean adoption, then the text says so! However, the woman's naming of her son Moses is purely symbolic, as with Joseph's naming of Jesus, '"because," she said, "I drew him out of the water"' (Exod. 2.10). There the word translated as 'I drew out' is *anaireō*, which Luke apparently took as adoption when he wrote Stephen's speech.

If the words 'became to her for a son' are an adoption formula, the closest thing to it elsewhere is Gen. 48.5 (Hebrew). There Jacob took his two grandsons, Ephraim and Manasseh, as his own: 'Your two sons...shall be mine; Ephraim and Manasseh shall be to me as Reuben and Simeon'. The Greek text agrees literally with the Hebrew. Another case in point is that of Esther. When her father and mother were dead, 'Mordecai had taken her to himself for a daughter' (Est. 2.7; Hebrew). The LXX reads: 'brought her up for a wife for himself'. The Esther passage is a report of an adoption, not an adoptive situation with a formula as in Gen. 48.5. In 1 Sam. 18.21 (Hebrew) Saul says to David, 'This day you shall become my son-in-law' (my trans.). Those who see an adoption formula in Jn 19.26, 'Behold your son', never come up with such a formula elsewhere in a more clearly adoptive situation.[19] As we have seen, Gen. 48.5 is the nearest to an adoption formula we know. There the adoptive father makes the declaration of the action, as did Pharaoh's daughter, the adoptive mother, when 'she took him [Moses] as her son'. The statement in Jn 19.27, 'The disciple took her into his own home', is not comparable because it says nothing about the disciple himself saying that she is his mother or her saying that he is her son.

In most of the passages mentioned there is some sort of formula stated or implied that involves a direct verbal response on the part of one or the other of the parties involved. The first formula appears in the Mishnah *Baba Batra*, 'This is my son' (*B. Bat.* 8.6). As I said above, there is nothing of the sort in the Joseph story. The passage in Jn 19.26-27 means no more than that Jesus asked the disciple whom he loved to

19. See, e.g., C.K. Barrett, *The Gospel According to St John* (Philadelphia: Westminster Press, 1978), p. 552. He says that in the phrase 'your son' the form of the words recalls formulae of adoption.

care for his mother after his death. The saying of Jesus may be taken to mean an especially close relationship like that between a mother and son, but there is nothing of adoption. Moreover, the disciple 'took her [Mary] into his own home'. Mary is not the subject of the action but the recipient of it. I know of no evidence for a son adopting a mother. And Luke, who regards Joseph as Jesus' father and who uses the word 'parents' with reference to Mary and Joseph, was not concerned with any of this stuff about adoption. And I suspect that Matthew didn't have any of it in mind either.

Temple/Jerusalem Motif

The motive behind Luke's composition of the last two pericopes, including Lk. 2.22-24, was primarily theological and geographical, not historical. The verses in Lk. 2.22-24 with respect to 'the law of the Lord' show only a general knowledge of Judaism, as those dealing with the census (Lk. 2.1-5) show only a general knowledge of Roman history. In each instance there is inaccuracy of detail and little connection with what follows. It seems reasonable to suspect, therefore, a geographical interest as the prevailing motive for the use of each account.

The story of the census served to have the birth of Jesus take place at Bethlehem. In like manner, the story of the purification and presentation in the temple served to get Jesus to Jerusalem, the center of Jewish politics and religion, early in his life.

The temple/Jerusalem motif plays a special part in the theological scheme of Luke–Acts. And there is no better tie-in with the rest of the Gospel than that motif. In light of what follows the first two chapters in Luke's Gospel and what is written in the early chapters of Acts, we can understand why Luke thought it was appropriate to begin his Gospel in Jerusalem with Zechariah in the temple and with the birth of John, Jesus' precursor.

In accordance with the temple/Jerusalem motif, Luke reverses the last two temptations of Jesus (Mt. 4.1-11; Lk. 4.1-13; see also Mk 1.12-13). By doing this, he places the temptation of Jesus to throw himself down from the pinnacle of the temple last. Thus, Luke makes the temple in Jerusalem the climactic scene in the temptation story. Moreover, from the central part of the Gospel onwards (Lk. 9.31, 51) Jerusalem is the focus of Jesus' journeys, 'because it is impossible for a prophet to be killed outside of Jerusalem' (Lk. 13.33; see also Lk. 13.22; 17.11; 19.11).

During the last week of Jesus' life, according to Luke, 'every day he was teaching in the temple' (Lk. 19.47; 21.37-38). In Luke the resurrection appearances of Jesus take place in and around Jerusalem (Lk. 24.13-49), whereas in Matthew they occur in Galilee (Mt. 28.11-20; see also Mk 16.1-8). (Recall Matthew's special interest in Galilee.) Only Luke reports the final words of Jesus to his disciples that 'repentance and forgiveness of sins is to be proclaimed in his name to all nations, beginning from Jerusalem' (Lk. 24.47). Then, according to Luke only, Jesus tells his disciples to 'stay here in the city [Jerusalem] until you have been clothed with power from on high' (i.e. the coming of the Holy Spirit; Lk. 24.49; see also Acts 1.8). And, finally, Acts begins where the Gospel of Luke ends—in Jerusalem—with Jesus' followers who receive the Holy Spirit as promised (Acts 1.4-5; 2.1-11; see also Lk. 24.49).

According to Luke, Jerusalem was the hub of God's people Israel from where Jesus' followers were to be witnesses for him 'in Jerusalem, in all Judea and Samaria, and to the ends of the earth' (Acts 1.8).

Chapter 9

LUKE'S POETIC SECTIONS (SONGS OR CANTICLES)

The obviously poetic sections of Luke's birth stories, usually referred to as canticles or songs, have been a source of debate and disagreement among scholars for more than a century. The canticles in the order of their occurrence are the Magnificat by Mary (Lk. 1.46-55), the Benedictus by Zechariah (Lk. 1.68-79), the Gloria in Excelsis by the heavenly host (Lk. 2.14) and the Nunc Dimittis by Simeon (Lk. 2.29-31).

These songs are the most difficult aspect of the birth stories, because a knowledge of Hebrew and Greek is helpful for the best understanding of their sources and composition. This study, therefore, is limited to some of the most important issues, so readers who want to study the canticles in more detail should consult the works referred to in this study.[1] First, let me say something about the songs in general and then make a few observations about individual songs.

Composition and Vocabulary

Brown discusses the four different theories that have been proposed about the composition of the canticles. (1) They were actually composed by those reported as their speakers, for example, the Benedictus by Zechariah. This theory originated before the era of critical scholarship. Because it is very unlikely that common people could spontaneously compose such poetry, no serious scholar today accepts this theory, according to Brown. And I agree. (2) Luke composed the canticles when he wrote the rest of his narratives. However, the canticles

1. See especially Brown, *Birth*, pp. 346-47 for various theories about the composition of the canticles and pp. 346-66, 456-66 and his extensive bibliographies. I am indebted to Brown for some of the things I say about the canticles. He and I had some communication about them and other aspects of the stories of Jesus' birth not long before his untimely death.

do not fit well with the surrounding narratives. If they were not there, we would never miss them. Indeed, as Brown says, 'The narrative would read more smoothly without them'. (3) 'The canticles were composed by Luke and added subsequently to an already existing (Lucan or pre-Lucan) narrative'. (4) 'The canticles were pre-Lucan or non-Lucan and were added by Luke to an already existing Lucan narrative'.[2]

Scholars generally, including Brown, have pointed out the Jewish characters and distinctively Jewish expressions that occur in the canticles. On the basis of that evidence, they conclude that the canticles were not composed by a Gentile Christian or Christians.

Now let us consider that point. Below is a list of specifically Jewish persons and expressions in Luke's stories of Jesus' birth. The references in italics occur in the canticles (sometimes from the Greek text): 'the sons of Israel' (Lk. 1.16); 'the house of Jacob' (Lk. 1.33); 'your people Israel' (*Lk. 2.32*); 'his servant Israel' (*Lk. 1.54*); 'the Lord God of Israel' (*Lk. 1.68*); 'the house of his servant David' (*Lk. 1.69*); 'in the city of David a Savior, who is Christ the Lord' (Lk. 2.11); 'God my Savior' (*Lk. 1.47*); 'to remember his holy covenant' (*Lk. 1.72*); 'our fathers' (*Lk. 1.55, 72*); and 'our father Abraham' (*Lk. 1.73*).

Here is a list of identical or similar distinctively Jewish names and expressions that occur in the body of Luke's Gospel or in Acts (from Greek texts): 'the sons of Israel' (Acts 5.21; 7.23, 37; 10.36); 'all the people of Israel' (Acts 4.10; 13.24); 'the God of this people Israel' (Acts 13.17); 'the peoples of Israel' (Acts 4.27); 'all the house of Israel' (Acts 2.36; 7.42); 'the twelve tribes of Israel' (Lk. 22.30); 'God has brought to Israel a Savior, Jesus' (Acts 13.23); 'the covenant which God gave to your fathers' (Acts 3.25); 'our father David, your servant' (Acts 4.25); 'the Lord God of Abraham and the God of Isaac and the God of Jacob' (Lk. 20.37); 'the God of Abraham and of Isaac and of Jacob, the God of our fathers' (Acts 3.13; 7.32); 'your fathers' (Lk. 11.47; Acts 3.25); 'the God of our fathers' (Acts 5.30; 22.14); 'their fathers' (Lk. 6.23, 26); 'Father, Lord of heaven and earth' (Lk. 10.21); 'our fathers' (Acts 7.11-12, 15; 13.17; 15.10; 26.6); 'children to Abraham' (Lk. 3.8); 'a son of Abraham' (Lk. 19.9); 'father Abraham' (Lk. 16.24, 30); 'a daughter of Abraham' (Lk. 13.16); and 'our father Abraham' (Acts 7.2).

2. Brown, *Birth*, pp. 346-47.

Besides the distinctively Jewish phrases that are the same or similar to ones used in the canticles and in the rest of Luke's birth stories, *hypsistos* (Lk. 1.32, 35, 76; 2.14) is a favorite word of Luke's, especially in his Gospel. *Hypsistos* ('Most High' or 'highest') is an epithet for God or for the heaven(s) as the place where he resides. In the Synoptic Gospels it occurs twice in Mark (Mk 5.7; 11.10) and once in Matthew (Mt. 21.9). Besides the four times in the birth stories, Luke uses *hypsistos* three times in the body of the Gospel (Lk. 6.35; 8.28; 19.38) and twice in Acts (Acts 7.48; 16.17).

Most of the typically Jewish expressions in the second list above occur in the speeches of characters in the book of Acts. Scholars generally agree that Luke himself composed those speeches and put them on the lips of the characters in his narrative. The typically Jewish expressions in the canticles in the first list above are on the lips of Luke's characters in the birth stories.

It seems highly unlikely that the canticles put in the mouths of several principal characters were sung spontaneously. Rather, as with the speeches in Acts and those in the writings of ancient historians, they stress the importance of the moment. Do these observations thus far give some evidence for believing that Luke, as a Gentile Christian, could have composed the canticles himself?

You might point out that the canticles are poetry. That is true. But there are other poetic sections in Luke's stories that are usually not set off as poetry in English translations. Observe, for example, the words of the angel to Zechariah, certainly composed by Luke (Lk. 1.13-17), which are actually set off as poetry in the Greek text. Indeed, we can even translate the first two verses into a rough form of poetry:

> Do not be afraid, Zechariah,
> for your prayer has been heard,
> and your wife Elizabeth will bear you a son
> and you will call his name John.
> And you shall have joy and rejoicing
> and many will rejoice at his birth.

Compare the poetic words of the angel to Mary, also surely composed by Luke himself, in Lk. 1.30-33 and 1.35 (my trans.):

> Do not fear, Mary, for you have found favor with God.
> And, behold, you will conceive in your womb and bear a son
> and you will call his name Jesus.
> He will be great and will be called a son of the Most High

> And the Lord God will give him the throne of his father David,
> And he will reign over the house of Jacob forever;
> And of his kingdom there will be no end.
>
> The Holy Spirit will come upon you
> And the power of the Most High will overshadow you.

Even the ordinary person Elizabeth is made to exclaim in poetry (Lk. 1.42):

> Blessed are you among women,
> And blessed is the fruit of your womb.

Compare the poetic lines of the LXX Judg. 5.24:

> Blessed among women be Jael,
> wife of Heber the Kenite.
> Of women [living] in tents,
> let her be most blessed.

Background and Authorship of the Canticles

With respect to the canticles, the problems most discussed are whether they were composed by Jews or by Jewish Christians and whether they were originally written in Hebrew, Aramaic, or Greek. Theories (3) and (4), outlined above, have much support among modern scholars.

The canticles have as their background hymns and psalms like those in Jewish literature from 200 BCE to 100 CE, for example, 1 Maccabees, Judith, *2 Baruch*, *4 Ezra*, and the *Thanksgiving Hymns* and the *War Scroll* from the Qumran community. Since the relative literature exists in either Semitic or Greek texts, the parallels between it and the Lukan canticles do not in themselves confirm the composition of the latter by Jews who spoke either Hebrew of Greek. Some scholars have proposed that the canticles were written by non-Christian Jews, others that they were the work of Jewish Christians. Brown favors 'Jewish Christian composition'.[3]

The Anawim

Following several other scholars, Brown believes the canticles came to Luke from a Jewish-Christian community of Anawim. Anawim, Brown says, means 'poor ones', people 'who could not trust in their own

3. Brown, *Birth*, pp. 347-55.

strength but had to rely in utter confidence upon God: the lowly, the poor, the sick, the down trodden, the widows and orphans'.[4]

There is considerable disagreement about the origins of the Anawim. Brown believes, however, that a good case can be made for the existence of such a group in postexilic Jewish history who thought of themselves as the remnant of Israel. They believed that they alone were the small remnant whom God would ultimately save. Certain poetic passages in the Old Testament identify the people of God and the remnant (Ps. 149.4; Isa. 49.13; 66.2). The Anawim, according to Brown, expressed their appeal for God's deliverance in psalms and hymns and worshipped with prayer and sacrifice.

According to Brown, Jewish Anawim who converted to Christianity might have looked upon Jesus as 'the fulfillment of their messianic expectations and have used hymns to hail what God had accomplished in Jesus'. Having already expressed his own view of the salvation brought by the conception and birth of Jesus, Luke took over the joyful expressions of the Anawim at the salvation brought by Jesus. But Luke 'applied them with a specificity that was not in their original purview'.

Brown believes that because of the way Luke (Acts 2.43-47; 4.32-37) depicts the Jewish Christian community at Jerusalem, the existence of Jewish Christian Anawim 'is not purely hypothetical'. It can be argued plausibly that 'Luke came upon these canticles in a Greek-speaking Jewish Christian community in an area influenced by Jerusalem Christianity'.[5]

In disagreement with Brown, Horsley maintains that no positive evidence points to a specific group of Anawim. Nor did Luke have in mind a particular class of pious people when he wrote the stories of Jesus' birth. This is true even for the narratives of Simeon and Anna that might indicate some kind of 'Temple Piety'. I am inclined to agree with Horsley on that point. According to Horsley, many of the Psalms used to support the theory of *anawim* 'appeal to God/Yahweh as the defender or refuge of the poor, oppressed *people of Israel/Judah* against the oppressive *foreign or domestic rulers*: Pss no. 9-10, 14, 147, 149 (cf. Pss. 82, 102-103, 113, 146)'. According to Horsley, Luke's infancy narratives are directed to the poor and lowly, who are 'the people of Israel in general', not a particular pious group, that 'is the social reality and context reflected' in the text of Luke. The stories 'are declared

4. Brown, *Birth*, pp. 350-51.
5. Brown, *Birth*, pp. 350-55.

repeatedly to be for the salvation, deliverance, or joy of the people (1:17, 68, 77; 2:10, 25, 32) of Israel (1:16, 33, 54; 2:25, 32)'. The proud, mighty and rich of Lk. 1.51-53, the enemies of Lk. 1.71, 74, are the ones from whom the lowly and hungry of Lk. 1.52-53, predominantly peasants, must be delivered, according to Horsley.[6]

No one was a greater defender of the poor, including widows, than Luke. The passage about the poor in the early church in Acts 1–4, which Brown points to in support of the Anawim theory, was composed by none other than Luke himself, at least in its present form. For the reasons just stated and others Goulder believes Luke composed the songs, primarily on the basis of Old Testament texts. Hannah's song was the model for Luke's Magnificat, according to Goulder, and I agree. Comparisons between the annunciation and visitations stories and the Magnificat show the similarity in type, language and theology.[7]

Horsley, as expected, believes the canticles are songs of liberation. They are, but in my opinion, he emphasizes the political and socio-economic aspects at the neglect of the religious. I agree with Horsley that women were more important in the Jesus movement from the beginning than was believed for far too long. However, that does not give one the liberty of reading more from a text than is there.

It is true that the four women foreshadow Mary in their roles in the 'production of the Messiah', as Horsley says. But in the texts I cited in Chapter 2 that deal with those women, without exception, God or the Holy Spirit initiated their roles in 'the production of the Messiah', as, indeed, he did with Mary. It is true, as Horsley says, that there is a 'significant lack of intervention by God' in the Old Testament stories of the women. However, it is also true that God would not have initiated the evil on the part of any one of them. Moreover, it is especially significant that in those Old Testament texts there is absolutely no reference to the Messiah.

As I have suggested, Matthew had to liberate Mary, as the last of the progenitors of the Messiah, as with the four women, from her guilt in order to assuage his critics who were charging the illegitimacy of his Messiah. It is not true that, using the 'traditions behind Matthew's genealogy' as a guide, 'not God's initiatives but women's actions proved the

6. Horsley, *Liberation*, pp. 63-68, quotations, pp. 67-68.

7. See Goulder, *Luke*, I, pp. 225-30.

means by which the people or its leadership were delivered', as Horsley asserts.[8]

If Matthew had in mind the kind of liberation Horsley defends, he would certainly more aptly have chosen Miriam, Deborah, Jael, Esther or Judith than the four mentioned. And in Luke it is not Mary herself who is the liberator or deliverer but her son, the Messiah. Of course, if the conception and delivery of the Messiah, though initiated by God, not Mary or Joseph, is responsible for the delivery of the people, than Mary can be regarded as a deliverer. A male could not have conceived and delivered the Messiah. If that had happened, it would be the greatest miracle of all in the stories of Jesus' birth.

Mary is greeted by Elizabeth as 'the mother of my Lord' (Lk. 1.43). Does 'Lord' in the Gospels of Matthew and Luke more often imply political and socioeconomic deliverance or religious salvation? Even in the Magnificat, put on the lips of Mary, her soul magnifies the Lord and rejoices in God her Savior (Lk. 1.46). God, not Mary, is the agent behind the scene.

Is it really true that the canticles are more in the nature of 'revolutionary songs of salvation' than 'pious prayers'? It may be that modern theologians have somewhat obscured the revolutionary nature of the songs of victory.[9] But at the same time, there is more than one kind of salvation (Hebrew, 'deliverance') or victory, though sometimes the kinds are intermingled, as they certainly closely are in the songs.

We must not underplay deliverance in the sense of religious salvation as conceived by the earliest followers of Jesus, including Luke, long before the rise of *modern* theologians. In order to help alleviate any bias I may have, let's look at some statistics with respect to theological terms in the vocabulary of the synoptic writers. *Sōzō* ('save')—Mark 15 × (all but one in healing contexts); Matthew 16 ×; Luke 17 ×; Acts 13 ×; *sōtēria* ('salvation)—Mark 11 ×; Matthew 0; Luke 4; Acts 6; *sōtērion* ('salvation')—Mark 0; Mt. 0; Luke 2 ×; Acts 1 ×; *sōtēr* ('savior')—Mark 0; Matthew 0; Luke 2 ×; Acts 2 ×. The synoptic writers in general were not concerned with salvation in the sense later Christians came to think of it. Luke has a greater emphasis on salvation in the theological sense than any other Gospel writer. Here are some specific texts.

8. Horsley, *Liberation*, pp. 87-88 and his notes.

9. Horsley, *Liberation*, p. 107.

In the Synoptic Gospels, including Luke, *sōzō* occurs mostly in the contexts of healing miracles. However, in Acts it is used at least eight times with the theological meaning of salvation (Acts 2.21, 47; 4.12; 11.14; 15.1, 11; 16.30, 31). *Sōtēria* occurs three times in the Benedictus (Lk. 1.69, 71, 77) and in Lk. 19.9 (only in Luke), where salvation comes to the house of Zacchaeus, who was 'rich' and 'a sinner'. In Acts *sōtēria* is used four times in the strictly theological sense (Acts 4.12; 13.26, 47; 16.17). *Sōtērion* is the word in Lk. 2.20 in the Nunc Dimittis and in Lk. 3.6 (all flesh seeing the salvation of God), in the context of John's eschatological preaching a baptism of repentance for the forgiveness of sins' (Lk. 3.3). *Sōtēr* occurs only in Luke's birth narratives (Lk. 1.47, Magnificat) and Lk. 2.11, 'a Savior, who is the Messiah, the Lord'. Is 'Lord' theological or political here? Acts has the answer to that question. God exalted Jesus as 'Leader and Savior that he might give repentance to Israel and forgiveness of sins' (Acts 5.31; see also Acts 13.23). The function of Savior applies to the Leader as well as to the Savior, namely, the giving of repentance and the forgiveness of sins. And we must not ignore the same function stated in the Benedictus: 'to give knowledge of salvation to his people by the forgiveness of their sins' (Lk. 1.77).

More could be said about Luke's emphasis on repentance, but I shall mention only several passages. Only Luke has the piece about repentance or perishing (Lk. 13.1-5). With respect to Horsley's emphasis on 'to all the people' (Lk. 2.10), to which he devotes a whole chapter, only Luke has the saying of the risen Jesus: 'Repentance and forgiveness of sins is to be proclaimed...to all nations' (Lk. 24.47). See also Acts 13.24: Before Jesus' coming into public life, 'John had already proclaimed a baptism of repentance to all the people of Israel'. And Acts 17.30: 'God...commands all people everywhere to repent'.

The above passages should serve to temper Horsley's view about Luke's meaning of liberation. Surely for Luke liberation was much more religious than political and socioeconomic. The religious factor should not be underestimated even in the songs.

The Magnificat

In my opinion Horsley is correct in saying that there is nothing eschatological in the Magnificat (Lk. 1.46-55). God has already acted in the baby Mary is carrying. Apocalyptic eschatology is really past history written in the future tense. With the exception of Lk. 1.48, 50, the verbs are past tense. I agree also with Horsley, against Brown and others, that there is no reference to the death and resurrection of Jesus in the Magnificat (see below).[10] Luke 1.48 is a flashback to 1.28, 'favored one' and to 1.42, 'Blessed are you among women'.

Luke 1.50 is a key verse: 'His mercy is for those who fear him from generation to generation'. The verse is a combination of Ps. 102.11: 'The Lord has strengthened his mercy to those who fear him' and Ps. 99.5: 'The Lord is good, his mercy is forever, and his truth to generation and generation'. As in Ps. 99.5, Luke has left his sentence verbless, and that makes the verse a key one in our study. It is the only verse that is immediately relevant (present tense implied) to Luke's special interest, as we shall see momentarily. 'Mercy' (*eleos*) is a favorite word of Luke's (Mark 0; Matthew 3 ×; Luke 6 ×, five of which appear in the birth stories). The sixth occurrence is in Lk. 10.37, where the Samaritan showed mercy on the Jew.

Horsley says that the revolution depicted in the Magnificat is 'not simply "political"' but 'social as well'. True, but it is also religious: 'His mercy is for those who fear him from generation to generation'. Mercy is not to be separated from the fear of the Lord. Mercy and the fear of God—those two, not politics, society or the economy—are the presuppositions behind the texts referred to by Horsley, with the possible exception of the *War Scroll* from Qumran.[11]

I wonder, really, if 'revolution' is not too strong a word to apply to the Magnificat. It seems to me 'deliverance' would be less loaded and sound more Jewish. If 'magnify' is the key word—else why do we call Mary's song the Magnificat?—then it is a joyful song of praise and thanksgiving like parts of many Old Testament psalms. Compare lines in the Magnificat with these lines from some psalms (from the LXX), and notice how similar they are. The psalms quoted are songs of praise and thanksgiving on the part of an individual for deliverance from some personal trouble. Psalm 33(34).3-4: 'My soul shall be praised in the Lord; let the humble hear and rejoice. Magnify the Lord with me, and let us exult his name together.' Psalm 34(35).9: 'My soul shall rejoice in the Lord; it shall delight in his salvation'. Psalm 12(13).5-6: 'But I trusted in your mercy; my heart shall rejoice in your salvation. I will

10. Horsley, *Liberation*, p. 113.

11. Horsley, *Liberation*, p. 113. Horsley mentions 1QM 14.10-11, part of a psalm giving thanks after battle.

sing to the Lord who has dealt bountifully with me, and I will sing a song to the name of the Lord Most High' (see also Ps. 68[69].30-31).

The Benedictus

With respect to the Benedictus (Lk. 1.68-79), let me make just a few points that I think should not be overlooked. Goulder says that the canticle is based on the Song of David, as the Magnificat is on Hannah's song. Most would agree, and so do I.[12]

Now let me point out a few places where Horsley emphasizes the political and socioeconomic factors to the neglect of the religious. With respect to the verb translated as 'has looked favorably' in the NRSV (Lk. 1.68), it is literally 'he has visited' (Greek verb *episkeptomai*). Horsley disagrees with Fitzmyer on 'the religious sense of the verb'. The passages in Exod. 4.31 and Ruth 1.6 do support Horsley's emphasis, as would Pss. 64.9; 79.14; and 105.4.[13]

But there are other psalms. 'You have visited [Greek verb *episkeptomai*] me...tried me with fire, and unrighteousness was not found in me' (Ps. 16.3). 'Come near to visit [*episkeptomai*] all the nations, do not pity all those who work lawlessness' (Ps. 58.5). Horsley says that in Ps. 110(111).9 sending redemption is in parallel with 'the sociopolitical "commanded his covenant,"' wonderful works, and giving food and land in the preceding verses. However, we should notice that the Lord 'gave food to those who fear him'. Moreover, 'his covenant' is 'all his commandments...done in truth and righteousness' (Ps. 110.7-8), in keeping with the covenant tradition in Exodus.

In Ps. 110 (111 in Hebrew) the psalmist is praising Yahweh for his great works. And his praise is given while 'in the company of the upright'. The psalmist praises God for his creation and 'the power of his works' in history, including especially the Hebrews' deliverance from Egypt and the covenant inherently linked with that event. We must remember that Hebrew history was basically religious history, including political and economic affairs. Kings were responsible to God, and God provided food for those who reverenced (feared) him and punished those who went astray. Indeed, wealth was not always regarded as evil. This is clear from the next psalm (Hebrew 112), which

12. For Goulder's treatment of the Benedictus, with which I agree, see his *Luke*, I, pp. 239-44.

13. Horsley, *Liberation*, p. 115.

most scholars regard as originally a part of the preceding one: 'The generation of the upright will be blessed. Wealth and riches are in their houses' (Ps. 112.2-3).

There is nothing in the text of Luke to indicate that the religious meaning of 'visiting' and 'redeeming' should not also be understood, if indeed the religious meaning is not primary. Visited, redeemed and raised a horn in the house of David is clearly a series of what God has already done in sending John (or Jesus, in the mind of Luke?). The horn of salvation in the house of David (Lk. 1.69; Greek) does not mean that 'redemption' (Lk. 2.38; 24.21) is to be taken only in the political and economic sense in Psalm 110(111) or in Lk. 1.69 and 24.21. Luke might well have put words in Zechariah's mouth similar to those in Sirach 51 (section in Hebrew not in Greek text): 'Give thanks to him who makes a horn to sprout for the house of David, for his mercy endures forever... He has raised up a horn for his people, praise for all his loyal ones. For the children of Israel, the people close to him. Praise the Lord!' (NRSV).

Would any devout Jew or Christian in the time of Luke, the ancient theologian, not have thought of including, to say nothing of stressing, the religious factor? Sometimes it seems as though Horsley thinks of Luke as a politician or an economist instead of a religious thinker.

Sometimes 'redemption' (*lytroō*, verb; *lytrōsis*, noun) is used with only the religious meaning, as in LXX Ps. 129.7, for example: 'With Lord is mercy, and with him is much redemption [*lytrōsis*]. And he will redeem [*lytrōsetai*] Israel from all its inequities.' In Isa. 1.18-31 there is a magnificent combination of the political and religious/moral elements in Isaiah's plea for the redemption of Jerusalem.

By calling attention to passages such as the ones I have mentioned, Horsley would have done much to prepare his readers for his conclusions, with which I concur. The forgiveness of sins in the Benedictus gives 'a new beginning for the people in living covenantal righteousness'. The Benedictus is 'not noticeably christological'. It praises God's salvation of the people comprehensively, whereby the sociopolitical and the religious elements are inseparable.[14] One does not expect such a conclusion after Horsley stresses too much, it seems to me, elements other than the religious, not only in the canticles but also in other places in the stories of Jesus' birth.

14. Horsley, *Liberation*, pp. 118-19.

Finally, on the subject of religion in the canticles, let me call attention again to several lines from *Psalms of Solomon* 17–18. These psalms were written after the destruction of Jerusalem by Pompey in 63 BCE and are among the clearest messianic passages in Jewish literature. The Jews had enough war and revolution and were looking for an age of peace. Although there are revolutionary passages in Psalm 17, here is what the psalmist says about the Messiah:

> And, taught by God, he will be a righteous king over them. And in his time there will be no unrighteousness among them, for all will be holy, and their king the Lord Messiah. For he will not put his trust in horse and rider and bow, nor will he multiply for himself gold and silver for war...the Lord himself is his king, the hope of anyone who has a powerful hope in God (17.36-38).

In *Psalms of Solomon* 18.1-7, which has the title 'A Psalm of Solomon about the Lord Messiah', there is not a word about revolution:

> Lord, your mercy is upon the works of your hands forever... Your ears listen to the begging of the poor who have hope. Your judgments are (made) with mercy over the whole earth, and your love is for the descendants of Abraham, sons of Israel... May God cleanse Israel [from sins] for the day of mercy with blessing, for the appointed day for raising up his Messiah. Blessed are those born in those days, to see the good things of the Lord which he will do for the coming generation; under the rod of discipline of the Lord Messiah in wisdom of spirit and righteousness and strength, to guide people in works of righteousness in the fear of God, to establish all of them before the Lord, a good generation in the fear of God in the days of mercy.

Compare the lines from that messianic psalm with the canticles, and notice the similarities in language and thought. This observation should caution us further about thinking too much of Jesus the 'Lord Messiah' (Acts 2.36) as the liberator of his people primarily from political and socioeconomic oppression.

Some Conclusions with Respect to the Canticles

I disagree with the view of Brown and others who favor a group of Anawim as the original composers of the canticles. With respect to the theory that they were composed by those who spoke them, Brown says, 'It is obviously unlikely that such finished poetry could have been composed on the spot by ordinary people'.[15] I agree wholeheartedly. How-

15. Brown, *Birth*, p. 346.

ever, according to Brown, the Anawim were the lowly, poor, sick, downtrodden, widows and orphans. They could not depend on their own strength but had to rely utterly upon God. Well, if people of that sort wrote such fine poetry, they would have been extraordinary 'ordinary people', would they not?

It might be argued, I suppose, as in times past, that the Holy Spirit could have inspired the 'ordinary people' or the Anawim to write such fine poetry. Luke himself believed that Zechariah 'was filled with the Holy Spirit' before he spoke the Benedictus (Lk. 1.67). According to Luke, 'the Holy Spirit rested on' Simeon. And 'Guided by the Spirit, Simeon came into the temple' (Lk. 1.25-27) before he said the Nunc Dimittis. We have observed that Luke says more about the Spirit and its power than any other Gospel writer. So if the Spirit came upon anyone, I'd place my bet on Luke himself. Here are some more characteristic Lukan expressions in his birth narratives.

enneuō ('motion', 'nod')—only in Lk. 1.62.
graphō ('write')—Mark 10 ×; Matthew 10 ×; Luke 20 ×; Acts 12 ×.
thaumazō ('wonder')—Mark 4 ×; Matthew 7 ×; Luke 13 ×; Acts 5 ×.
parachrēma ('immediately')—Mark 0; Matthew 2 ×: Luke 10 ×; Acts 6 ×.
phobos ('fear') coming upon—only Lk. 1.12, 65; for similar expressions see also Lk. 5.26; 7.16; 8.37; Acts 5.5, 11; 19.17.
eulogeō ('bless', with God as object)—only Lk. 1.64; 2.28; 24.53.
laleō ('tell', 'speak', 'say')—Mark 21 ×; Matthew 26 ×; Luke 31 ×; Acts 59 ×.
perioikeō ('live near')—only in Lk. 1.65.
oreinē ('hill country')—only in Lk. 1.39, 65.
hrēmata tauta ('these words')—Lk. 1.65; 2.19; 24.11; Acts 5.32; 10.44; 13.42; 16.38.
hrēma touto ('this word')—Lk. 2.15; 9.45 (2 ×); 18.34.
tithēmi en kardia ('put' or 'lay in heart')—Lk. 1.66; 21.14; Acts 5.4.
cheir kyriou ('hand of the Lord')—only in Lk. 1.66; Acts 11.21; 13.11.
sunchairō ('rejoice with')—only in Lk. 1.58; 15.6, 9.[16]

Luke's Role in the Composition of the Songs

Not everyone agrees about whether Luke was a Gentile or Jewish Christian. Scholars, however, generally agree that Luke, no matter about his ethnic and religious background, was well educated in Hellenistic culture and was very familiar with the language of the Septuagint. But how about the readers for whom his two works were intended? Were they

16. Many more could be given. See Goulder's lists in vol, I, pp. 218-20, 234-37, 244-46, 253-55, 261-64, 268-69, 272-73, and following pages.

mostly Jews or Gentiles? If Theophilus, the person mentioned in Luke's prefaces (Lk. 1.3; Acts 1.1), represents Gentiles, then probably most of Luke's readers were Gentiles, perhaps still in the process of becoming converts to Christianity. Such Gentiles were undoubtedly associated with Jewish synagogues and therefore, like Luke, would be reading and studying the Jewish scriptures in their Greek version(s). Through the study of such versions, persons in the synagogue would be familiar with the distinctively Jewish persons and characteristic expressions Luke used both in the Gospel and in Acts. So, could Luke have written the Gospel that bears his name, along with the stories of Jesus' birth, including the canticles, for such converts?

It is true that the canticles do seem to be poorly adapted to their contexts. On the other hand, the canticles all have their setting in Judea, in which the cities of Bethlehem and Jerusalem were located. The Magnificat (Lk. 1.46-55), was uttered by Mary in 'a Judean town in the hill country' (Lk. 1.39). The Benedictus (Lk. 1.68-79) was spoken by the priest Zechariah either from his home in the Judean town where he lived or in the temple in Jerusalem. The multitude of angels (Lk. 2.13-14) spoke or sang their praise to God in the vicinity of Bethlehem (see Lk. 2.8: 'in that region'). And Simeon uttered his parting blessing of Jesus, the Nunc Dimittis (Lk. 2.29-32), in the temple in Jerusalem. Remember that Luke has a special interest in Judea and Jerusalem.

The speakers of the canticles, then, according to Luke, are the first witnesses to Jesus the Messiah in Jerusalem and Judea. Although Luke may not adeptly have adapted the canticles to their contexts, they serve his theological and geographical purposes well. According to Luke, when the Holy Spirit has come upon the first followers of Jesus, they will be his 'witnesses in Jerusalem, in all Judea and Samaria, and to the ends of the earth' (Acts 1.8).

We have learned that Luke adapted whatever material he had from whatever sources to his own literary style and his theological and/or geographical purposes. Evidence hardly permits us to go beyond that in trying to resolve the many problems with respect to the canticles and other features of Luke's infancy narratives. However, the case for their composition by Luke himself is extremely strong.

The Jewishness of the Canticles

By looking at the table of parallels in Chapter 6 above, you will observe that many of the contrasts between John and Jesus occur in the canticles. There seems little doubt, then, that Luke used the canticles as part of his scheme of emphasizing the superiority of Jesus over John. But in doing so he did not take away a bit of their Jewishness. Any reference to Jesus must be read into them. No matter what we have said or might say about the composition, origin and substance of the canticles, their theology as well as their language is thoroughly Jewish, but Lukanized.

In the Magnificat (Lk. 1.46-53) Mary is made to sing: 'My soul magnifies the Lord, and my spirit rejoices in God my Savior'.

Here Lord and God are in parallel, so it is God, not Jesus, who is her Savior. Compare 'You are God, my Savior' (Ps. 24.5; see also Ps. 23.15). God is the Mighty One who has done great things for her. Throughout the canticle the 'he' is God. Indeed, if thoughts about Jesus were not read into the canticle, no one would suspect that it had a thing to say about Jesus or about anything specifically Christian. Things Christian must be read into the Magnificat.

Surely, then, I cannot agree with Stephen Farris that the decisive help for Israel (see Lk. 1.54) 'is best explained as the coming of Jesus Christ and, more specifically, his death and resurrection'.[17] Christology must be read into the text; it cannot be read from the text.

In the Benedictus (Lk. 1.68-79), put on the lips of Zechariah, father of John, the 'child' is John who is to be the forerunner of the Davidic Messiah. But there is no hint in the hymn itself that Jesus is to be that Messiah. And it is 'by the tender mercy of our God', not Jesus, that all the things in the hymn are to take place. Again, anything Christian must be read into the hymn.

The same is true for the Nunc Dimittis (Lk. 2.29-32), uttered by the 'righteous and devout' Simeon. If we did not have Luke's statement that he took the baby Jesus 'in his arms and praised God', we could find no reference whatsoever to Jesus or anything Christian in Simeon's canticle. We would take it as a typical Hebrew (Jewish) psalm or hymn like those in the Old Testament or the Qumran hymns (see, e.g., LXX Ps. 98.2-3 and LXX Isa. 40.5-6; 49.6, 9; 46.13; 52.7-10). Consider, for example, Ps. 98.2-3 (LXX):

> The Lord has made known his salvation before the Gentiles;
> He has revealed his righteousness.

17. *The Hymns of Luke's Infancy Narratives: Their Origin, Meaning and Significance* (JSNTSup, 141; Sheffield: JSOT Press, 1985), p. 126.

> He has remembered his mercy to Jacob,
> And his truth to the house of Israel; All the ends of the earth shall see the salvation of our God.

See also LXX Isa. 40.5; 46.13; 49.6, 9; 52.10 (Hebrew).

The stories of Jesus' birth are interesting, interrelated and perplexing. They raise many problems. That Jesus was born seems certain enough. And that he was born as a human being may well have been one of the main things Matthew and Luke wanted to say. Paul had twice expressed that fact in his own simple way. As God's Son, Jesus 'was descended from David, according to the flesh' (Rom. 1.3). And at just the right time, 'God sent his Son, born of a woman, born under the law' (Gal. 4.4), that is, born as a Jew.

If we leave out Paul's theology (Jesus as God's Son), we have Jesus' human birth, 'born of a woman' and 'according to the flesh'. That Jesus was a Jew, 'born under the law', is not disputable. These are facts of history as we find them also in the stories of Jesus' birth. Perhaps Jesus was a descendant of David.

Professor J.K. Elliott has stated the matter succinctly: 'For all their apparent historicizing and verisimilitude, the Christmas story provides us with no more real facts about the historical Jesus than Paul himself does'.[18]

The rest of the birth stories express religious truths and theological convictions of Matthew and Luke in beautiful and edifying legends, myths and poetry.

18. J.K. Elliott, *Questioning Christian Origins* (London: SCM Press, 1982), p. 17.

BIBLIOGRAPHY

Babbitt, Frank C., *et al.*, *Plutarch's Moralia with an English Translation* (LCL; 16 vols.; London: Heinemann; New York: Putnam's Sons, 1927–1969).

The Babylonian Talmud (trans. I. Epstein *et al.*; 17 vols.; London: Soncino, 1935–52).

Barrett, C.K., *The Gospel According to St. John* (Philadelphia: Westminster Press, 1978).

Benoit, P., ' *"Non erat eis locus in diversorio" (Lc 2,7)*', in A. Descamps and A. de Halleux (eds.), Mélanges Beda Rigaux (Gembloux: Duculot, 1970), pp. 173-86.

Brown, Raymond E., *The Birth of the Messiah: A Commentary on the Infancy Narratives in the Gospels of Matthew and Luke* (New York: Doubleday, 1993).

Campbell, E.F., Jr, *Ruth* (AB, 7; Garden City, NY: Doubleday, 1975).

Colson, F.H., and G.H. Whitaker, *Philo with an English Translation* (LCL; 10 vols.; London: Heinemann; New York: Putnam's Sons, 1929–52).

Conybeare, F.C., *Philostratus: The Life of Apollonius of Tyana with an English Translation* (LCL; 2 vols.; London: Heinemann; New York: Putnam's Sons, 1921, 1926).

Deissmann, Adolf, *Light from the Ancient East* (trans. L.R.M. Strachan; New York: Doran, 1927).

Elliott, J.K., *Questioning Christian Origins* (London: SCM Press, 1982).

Encyclopaedia Judaica (ed. Cecil Roth *et al.*; 16 vols.; Jerusalem: Keter Publ. Co.; New York: Macmillan, 1972).

Farris, Stephen, *The Hymns of Luke's Infancy Narratives: Their Origin, Meaning and Significance* (JSNTSup, 141; Sheffield: JSOT Press, 1985).

Fitzmyer, Joseph A., *The Gospel According to Luke* (AB, 28a; 2 vols.; Garden City, NY: Doubleday, 1981).

—'The Virginal Conception of Jesus in the New Testament', *TS* 34 (1973), pp. 541-75.

Freed, Edwin D., 'The Women in Matthew's Genealogy', *JSNT* 29 (1987), pp. 3-19.

Ginzberg, Louis, *The Legends of the Jews* (7 vols.; Phildelphia: Jewish Publication Society of America, 1959–68).

Goulder, Michael D., *Luke: A New Paradigm* (JSNTSup, 20; 2 vols.; Sheffield: JSOT Press, 1989).

Gundry, R.H., *Matthew: A Commentary on his Literary and Theological Art* (Grand Rapids: Eerdmans, 1982).

Hawkins, J.C., *Horae Synopticae* (Grand Rapids: Baker Book House, 1968).

Hennecke, E., *New Testament Apocrypha* (ed. W. Schneemelcher; trans. R. McL. Wilson; 2 vols.; London: Lutterworth, 1963–64).

Horsley, Richard A., *The Liberation of Christmas: The Infancy Narratives in Social Context* (New York: Crossroad, 1989).

Marshall, I.H., *The Gospel of Luke* (Grand Rapids: Eerdmans, 1978).

The Midrash Rabbah (trans. H. Freedman *et al.*; 10 vols.; London: Soncino, 1939).

Moulton, James H., and George Milligan, *The Vocabulary of the Greek Testament* (London: Hodder & Stoughton, 1949).

Nock, A.D., 'Paul and the Magus', in F.J. Foakes Jackson, K. Lake and H.J. Cadbury (eds.), *The Beginnings of Christianity* (5 vols.; London: Macmillan, 1922–42), V, pp. 164-88.

Nolland, N.J., 'What Kind of Genesis Do We Have in Matt 1.17?', *NTS* 42 (1996), pp. 463-71.

Novum Testamentum Graecae (Neu bearbeitete Auflage, 26; Stuttgart: Deutsche Bibelstiftung, 1979 [1898]).

Oldfather, W.A., *Epictetus: The Discourses as Reported by Arrian, the Manual, and Fragments with an English Translation* (LCL; 2 vols.; Cambridge, MA: Harvard University Press; London: Heinemann; New York: Putnam's Sons, 1956 [1928]).

Perrin, Bernadotte, *Plutarch's Lives with an English Translation* (LCL; 11 vols.; Cambridge, MA: Harvard University Press; London: Heinemann, 1919–49).

Rolfe, J.C., *Suetonius with an English Translation* (LCL; 2 vols.; London: Heinemann; New York: Macmillan; Cambridge, MA: Harvard University Press, 1979 [1914]).

Schaberg, J., *The Illegitimacy of Jesus* (San Francisco: Harper & Row, 1987).

Schürer, Emil, *The History of the Jewish People in the Age of Jesus Christ*, III.1 (rev. and ed. G. Vermes, F. Millar and M. Goodman; Edinburgh: T. & T. Clark, 1986).

Thackeray, H.St.J., Ralph Marcus and Louis Feldman, *Josephus with an English Translation* (LCL; 9 vols.; London: Heinemann; New York: Putnam's Sons; Cambridge, MA: Harvard University Press, 1926–65).

Wright, R.B., 'Psalms of Solomon', pp. 639-70 in *The Old Testament Pseudepigrapha* (ed. J.H. Charlesworth; 2 vols.; Garden City, NY: Doubleday, 1983, 1985).

INDEXES

INDEX OF REFERENCES

OLD TESTAMENT

OTHER ANCIENT TEXTS

INDEX OF AUTHORS